MAKING FRIENDS
(& MAKING THEM *COUNT*)

EM GRIFFIN

INTERVARSITY PRESS
DOWNERS GROVE, ILLINOIS 60515

InterVarsity Press is the book-publishing division of InterVarsity Christian Fellowship, a student movement active on campus at hundreds of universities, colleges and schools of nursing. For information about local and regional activities, write Public Relations Dept., InterVarsity Christian Fellowship, 6400 Schroeder Rd., P.O. Box 7895, Madison, WI 53707-7895.

Distributed in Canada through InterVarsity Press, 860 Denison St., Unit 3, Markham, Ontario L3R 4H1, Canada.

Excerpt on page 17 from Communication: The Transfer of Meaning by Don Fabun. Copyright © 1968, Kaiser Aluminum & Chemical Corporation. Reprinted with permission of Glencoe Publishing Co., a Division of Macmillan, Inc.

Excerpt from Country: ©1984 Buena Vista Distributor Co., Inc.

Excerpt from Hughes Mearns, Creative Power. Courtesy of Dover Publications, Inc.

Excerpt from The Chosen: Copyright ©1967 by Chaim Potok. Reprinted by permission of Simon & Schuster.

Excerpt from: "Show Me" by Alan J. Lerner & Frederick Loewe. Copyright ©1956 by Alan J. Lerner & Frederick Loewe. Copyright renewed. Chappell & Co., Inc., owner of publication and allied rights. International Copyright Secured. All rights reserved. Used by permission.

A previous version of chapter two first appeared in Today's Christian Woman Fall 1980 and Winter 1980-81.

A previous version of chapter three first appeared in Leadership (Summer 1985) under the title "What Motivates You?"

All Scripture quotations, unless otherwise indicated, are from the Holy Bible, New International Version. Copyright © 1973, 1978. International Bible Society. Used by permission of Zondervan Bible Publishers.

Cover cartoon: Reprinted by permission of Jerry Marcus

ISBN 0-87784-996-X

Printed in the United States of America

Library of Congress Cataloging in Publication Data

Griffin, Emory A.
    Making friends & making them count.

    Bibliography: p.
    1. Friendship—Religious aspects—Christianity.
2. Interpersonal relations—Religious aspects—
Christianity.   I. Title.
BV4647.F7G74   1987   241'.676   87-2619
ISBN 0-87784-996-X

17	16	15	14	13	12	11	10	9	8	7	6	5	4	3	2	1
99	98	97	96	95	94	93	92	91	90	89	88	87				

For my friends—
starting with
Sharon, Jim and Jean

Introduction

Last night I watched the Chicago Bears on "Monday Night Football." The video coverage was superb. Isolated close-ups, instant replays and diagrammed analyses of successful plays gave me a much better insight into the game than I'd get sitting in the stadium. But the network announcers were too balanced for my taste. I'm a partisan, a rabid supporter, a fan. So I turned the sound all the way down and listened to the play-by-play coverage on our local radio station. Those guys are "homers." They don't care who wins as long as it's the Bears. The two-channel approach gave me the best of both worlds—precise description and booster excitement.

I hope that's your experience reading this book. I wanted to write a keen account of what goes on in face-to-face interaction. A clear understanding of the dynamics in one-on-one relationships can make our interpersonal communication more effective.

But I'm not content with detached analysis. I believe that God gave us the gift of communication so we could get close to others. I'm for the home team. You'll find that the further you read in the book, the more my bias toward close friendship leaks out. If you want the full blast of advocacy, start with the last chapter. I kid my wife about how she often reads the end of a novel first. If you've been burned by friends before, or are fearful of risking closeness, jumping ahead to the end might be a good idea. If not, I think you'll appreciate the gradual development from what *is* to what *could be.*

You'll catch glimpses of some of my friendships throughout these pages. Let's start with Gordon. He stopped by this weekend to confirm the date of a breakfast meeting at an upcoming InterVarsity Christian Fellowship conference. We'll be leading a joint discussion on the topic of the Christian and money—an area of mutual struggle. It took thirty seconds to clarify the date. The next thirty minutes was a jumble of shared feelings, easy laughter, mild argument, request for prayer and recounting of old stories. It seemed like no time at all. This morning in church he confirmed what we both knew. Making plans was just an excuse for spending time together. Gordon is my friend.

"Lucky man," you say—and no doubt I am. But making friends and making them count is more than the luck of the draw or the fickle finger of fate. Early Greek philosophers debated the issue as to whether speaking effectiveness is a knack or an art. They concluded that it's more than the gift-of-gab. Interpersonal communication has a conscious body of knowledge that can be mastered and applied. Friendship is an art.

This book surveys the state of the art. For those who want to go deeper into a given topic of interpersonal communication, I've included a bibliography in the back with the best book I know in each field. Sometimes these are written by Christians; more often they are by writers claiming no theological intent. I believe that all truth is God's truth, wherever it's found.

Because of the personal nature of the subject, I've included three self-scoring personality tests in the early chapters of the book. I hope they'll provide insight into your preferred way of interacting with others. I'd be scared if you let a paper-and-pencil test talk you into anything. But I think the results can show you ways you might want to alter your behavior toward others. I'm committed to the idea that change is possible. So when you run across one of these diagnostic surveys, I urge you to invest the few minutes necessary to play the game. Self-understanding is the protein that makes growth possible.

You'll also find a number of cartoons interspersed throughout these pages. Readers of *The Mind Changers*[1] and *Getting Together*[2] have assured me that the artwork is the best part of my books. (Why don't I feel reassured?) I believe that the perceptive cartoonist is the closest thing we have to a modern-day prophet, so I include them for their bite. But I also am committed to the belief that God wants us to take him, but not ourselves, seriously. So I include them for fun as well.[3] Enjoy.

Sometimes the authors of communication books include a page or two of personal biography coupled with a casual snapshot. I played with this approach, but my trial run seemed a bit pretentious and self-serving. I want you to know me but would rather emerge naturally as I draw on my own story in the context of each chapter. By the last chapter you'll have a mind's-eye image of Em Griffin much more valid than any Kodak print.

Throughout the book I promote dialog over one-way communication. It would be unfair for me to want you to care about me and my ideas if you didn't have a chance to tell me your story. I've arranged with InterVarsity Press to provide a response card at the back of this book. I'd love it if you'd take a few minutes and tell me who you are, why you're reading the book or how you feel about things I've said. Who knows, you might even get a letter back. But for now I hope you'll plunge into the world of making friends with a strong commitment to making them count.

1

THE RULES
OF THE
GAME

*Interpersonal communication
is a process.*

I THINK IN PICTURES. When I hear the word *city*, I call up images of sky-scrapers surrounded by a loop of elevated train tracks, men and women in business suits walking fast, streets clogged with cars, money changing hands. That's how I picture Chicago.

Mention the term *risk* and my mind sifts through snapshots of skydivers plunging toward the earth, commodity traders in the pit betting their bankroll on the future price of soybeans, a college student haltingly confessing a private wound to his professor.

Mathematicians and philosophers urge us to think in pure abstractions. But I find in myself a great resistance to staying on a theoretical level. If someone speaks of *predestination*, I immediately picture a puppet on a string or a robot being controlled by a sinister-looking man sitting at a panel filled with electronic dials. Theologians would be quick to tell me that my images do violence to the concept of predestination—and undoubtedly they do. But most folks respond to the pictures, not the words.

Perhaps that's why God took "human form" (Phil 2:5-8). He understood our need for a living model. In Jesus we can see an enfleshed Deity, the visible image of the invisible God. I need that. My guess is that most of us do.

All of this bears on the contents of this book. I can tell you that interpersonal communication is *the process of creating unique shared meaning*. I believe it and would go to the wall defending each concept I've built into that definition. But that phrase would simply vegetate unless I could help you build up a structure of pictures to make it come to life. So in this opening chapter I'll try to describe interpersonal communication using a series of metaphors, talking about what could be vague in terms of familiar, concrete images.

Most of us play and watch a variety of games. Therefore I'll illustrate what interpersonal communication is, and what it's not, by referring to different sports and parlor games. When I'm through, I hope the phrase *a process of creating unique shared meaning* will have come alive through an album of mental photographs.

Communication as Bowling

Bowling is the number one participation sport in the United States. Although it doesn't have the glamour of tennis or the addictive quality of jogging, more people try to convert a ten-pin spare than work on their backhand or run in a 5K race. A bowling model of message delivery is probably the most widely held view of communication as well. That's unfortunate.

In this model the bowler is the sender. He addresses the pins—the target audience. He delivers the ball—the message. It rolls down the lane—the channel for the message. Clutter in the lane/channel can deflect the ball/ message. When it strikes the passive pins/audience, it has a certain predictable effect. This communication model places emphasis on smooth delivery of a message. The speaker/bowler must take care to select a precisely crafted message/ball and practice diligently to deliver it the same way every time. That makes sense if the target listeners are static pins uniformly set to receive the message.

Of course life isn't that simple. People aren't identical, interchangeable listeners quietly waiting to be bowled over by our words. They come in all shapes and sizes and are devilishly unpredictable. In real life the same message will have a different effect on different people at different times. Communication training that emphasizes the content of the message to the neglect of other factors won't work.

The bowling analogy also fails because the pins don't roll the ball back at the bowler. In the days before automatic pin-spotters, I somehow angered the pin boy, and he returned my ball with spit in the finger holes. Welcome to real-life interpersonal communication. It's messy. The audience usually isn't passive. It's very much involved. Communication is more than just a speaker's action. This realization has led some to propose an interactive model for communication. Tennis or Ping-Pong come to mind.

Communication as Ping-Pong

Unlike bowling, Ping-Pong can't be a solo game. It takes two to play. That fact alone makes it a better communication illustration. One party puts the conversational ball in play; the other positions himself to receive it. It takes more concentration and skill to field the ball cleanly than it does to serve it. The speaker/server knows where the message is going. The listener/receiver doesn't. Like a verbal message, the ball may appear straightforward, yet have a deceptive spin. The more knowledge the receiver has of the server's past performance and habits, the better he or she is able to anticipate how the ball will bounce.

Ping-Pong is a back-and-forth game. Players switch roles continuously. One moment the person behind the paddle is an initiator. A second later he's a reactor, gauging the effectiveness of his shot by the way the ball comes back. The repeated adjustment essential for good play is a close parallel to the feedback process in good interpersonal communication. But there are still three flaws inherent in the table-tennis analogy which make it come up short.

In the first place Ping-Pong is played in a controlled environment. The platform is stable, the bounce is true, the ball's not deflected by the wind.

Mordillo/Camera Press

In contrast, most face-to-face communication occurs in a storm of distraction.

The second defect is that the game is played with one ball, which at any given time is headed in a single direction. That's like the game Password where one player says a word and then the other responds with another word. Back and forth they go in a ritualized turn-taking fashion until communication is successful. A true model of interpersonal encounter would have both people sending and receiving balls at the same time.

The other problem is that Ping-Pong is a competitive game. Someone wins, someone loses. In successful dialog, both people win.

Communication as Charades

I think the game of charades better captures the simultaneous and cooperative nature of interpersonal communication. A charade is neither an action, like a strike in bowling, nor an interaction, like a point in Ping-Pong. It's a transaction.

Charades is a team game. While a team may be competing against other teams, the actual play is cooperative. One member draws a slogan or title from a batch of possibilities and then tries to depict it visually for teammates in a minidrama. The actor's job is to get at least one partner to say the exact words on the slip of paper. Of course the actor is prohibited from talking out loud. Rather he must pantomime a slice of life that will cause the audience to create the words in their minds.

Suppose you drew the saying, "God helps them who help themselves." You might want to argue the theology of the statement, but that's not the point. Your goal is to get other people to come up with mental pictures that will cause them to utter identical words. For *God* you might try folding your hands and gazing upward. For *helps* you could act out helping someone with the dishes or with changing a tire. Pointing at a number of imaginary people may elicit the response *them* for the third word. At this stage someone may well fill in the gaps and shout out with glee—"God helps them who help themselves." Success.

Interpersonal communication, like charades, is an ongoing creative process of helping others build images in their minds. Communication between us begins when there is some overlap between two images, yours and mine. The more overlap, the more communication. But even when the images are congruent, chances are that communication is only partial. For each of us may ascribe different meanings to identical images. "God helps them who help themselves" may be a comforting theological truth to some

"I have a pet at home."

"Oh, what kind of a pet?"

"It is a dog."

"What kind of a dog?"

"It is a St. Bernard."

"Grown up or a puppy?"

"It is full grown."

"What color is it?"

"It is brown and white."

"Why didn't you say you had a full-grown, brown and white St. Bernard as a pet in the first place?"

but a cynical mockery to others. To one, "a brown and white St. Bernard" may be man's best friend. To others, it could refer to a shedding, chewing, drooling, nonhousebroken pest. It's only when the emotional impact of the images matches up that true communication has occurred. A tall order.

Sometimes a kind of mass click will take place within a group or within a subculture. Thousands of people watch the same home run at a stadium or the same scene in a movie and share similar reactions. But interpersonal communication is different from that. The label *interpersonal* is appropriate only when the special meaning is shared by just two people. That's why my definition speaks of a unique shared meaning. It's a private transaction.

Ten Rules of Interpersonal Communication

A sensitive observer of the human scene who often watches charades would reach some conclusions about the rules of the game—not only the formal written rules which govern the play but also the unvoiced, informal laws of behavior. The same is true in interpersonal communication. There are rules of the game to be deciphered by anyone who cares to watch. I think charades is an apt model of one-on-one encounter.

I'll list ten axioms that have become commonplace to those who study interpersonal communication. Charade buffs may be intrigued to see how their game illustrates these principles. The ten rules also introduce the content of each chapter in this book.

Interpersonal communication is a process.[1] No single snapshot does it justice. Freeze frame any given instant of the process, and you've told a lie. Only an account of the ebb and flow mirrors the truth. Like charades, communication is best seen as an ongoing transaction.

A game of charades can be a zoo. The actor may start with an orderly plan. But as soon as the timer says "Go!" the skit turns chaotic. The actor's motions elicit responses from the audience which in turn have an impact on the next bit of pantomime. Every action is both a cause and an effect. It's a dynamic, swirling process, neither simple nor very predictable. Success requires that each player send and receive messages at the same time. I've tried to illustrate that truth through the three communication models in this chapter—bowling, Ping-Pong and charades.

Interpersonal communication starts with the self.[2] Polaroid photography was just coming on the scene when I was a teen-ager. I went to a party where a camera buff brought his new toy—a Polaroid camera with a timed delay so a guy could take his own picture. He did. In fact he took two while he acted out a charade. One was blurred and out of focus. The other was sharp—facial features standing out in bold relief against the background.

Some people have a self-concept like the first fuzzy snapshot. Their murky image leaves them ill-equipped to play in a fast-paced game where decisiveness is an asset. The first part of chapter two deals with ways to bring our self-image into focus. Of course it's possible to have a highly developed self-portrait and still think we have a bad case of the uglies. I discuss self-esteem in the second part of chapter two and give suggestions for raising that evaluation. A team of players confident that they'll do well probably will. That's also true when it isn't a game. Our image of how we stack up has a major impact on our actions around other people.

The chances for effective communication increase as people become aware of their motives for getting together.[3] Folks who like to play charades are drawn to the game for different reasons. Some crave a sense of accomplishment as they decipher obscure quotations. Others want the recognition that comes from being on stage. Many desire the sense of camaraderie that springs from joint activity with others. Chapter three deals with motivation. Humans who catch a glimpse of why they are communicating have a leg up on those who merely react. Socrates claimed that the unexamined life is not worth living. I'm not sure I'd go that far. But our communication has an added zing when we have a handle on the forces drawing us toward interpersonal encounter.

People communicate to reduce uncertainty.[4] The purpose of the game of charades is to move from ambiguity to certainty, to bring order out of chaos. At the start of a round, there is complete ignorance. The phrase or slogan could be anything. By the time a successful conclusion is reached there is total predictability. We've eliminated all other options. We do the same thing in perceiving our world. We're bombarded by a myriad of sensory stimuli through our ears, eyes, touch, smell and taste. We desperately want to make some kind of sense out of it all so that our world becomes a safe, predictable place. Sometimes in our quest for certainty we simplify and stereotype people to make them seem less complicated than they really are. Chapter four takes a look at how we try to figure out other people with an eye toward knowing how they'll treat us.

Words don't mean things, people mean things.[5] I'll never forget the time my young daughter was trying to act out "The Dick Van Dyke Show." She repeatedly pretended to walk briskly while holding something in her hand. We guessed all sorts of things, but never came close. When we hit the time limit she scolded us for being dense. "Why didn't you get it? I had my sandwich and was going to Ann's house for lunch. *Ann* for Dick *Van* Dyke. It was so easy."

Right. The same pantomime meant one thing to Sharon and something very different to the rest of us. Language is the same way. The meaning doesn't reside in the word; it's in the people. Chapter five deals with language and how to listen to it to catch what it means to the other person.

You cannot not communicate.[6] Charades is a nonverbal game. The whole idea is to use gestures to get people to create the right words. That's the intention. But a whole slew of attitudes come across that the actor doesn't plan. He can't help it. They just leak out through posture, facial expression, pace and so on. It's the same in real-life communication. Interpersonal distance, body position, eye contact, tone of voice and many other non-verbal cues carry a big hunk of the communication load. Chapter six will investigate the major channels of nonverbal communication.

Without identification, there is no communication.[7] Most of us like others who are like us. People who share similar personalities, background experiences and values are ahead of the game in charades. Not only do they win more often than diverse teams, they also enjoy each other's company more. Similarity is just one of a number of forces that attract two people to each other—but it's a crucial one. Chapter seven explores the whole batch. While affinity doesn't guarantee effective discourse, its absence makes unique shared meaning an idle dream.

To reveal oneself openly and honestly takes the rawest kind of courage.[8] I once played charades when a woman drew the title of a famous painting by Marcel Duchamps, *Nude Descending a Staircase*. She read the words, blushed slightly and then turned pensive. She began considering her options. She could safely act out the phrase word by word, or she could portray the whole concept by walking down imaginary steps while pretending to disrobe. Those of us who already knew what she had drawn could see her balancing the benefit of quick success versus the cost of potential embarrassment. She chose the risky option.

Just as soon as the timekeeper said "Go!" she made exaggerated stepping motions and reached for the top button of her blouse. Simultaneously two players shouted out, "Nude Descending a Staircase!" The whole thing took three seconds. Risk is the topic of chapter eight. Most folks weigh carefully the cost of being vulnerable. Trust between people makes the risk of transparency tolerable. Self-disclosure, in turn, enhances trust. These two work together in a vital circle to draw people close together.

Communication is irreversible and unrepeatable.[9] Every verbal and nonverbal interchange is unique. It happens only once and then is etched in stone. We can't take it back or rewrite the script. I've seen charade players wipe off an imaginary chalk board to try to get their teammates to blot out early misconceptions. It seldom works.

It's even harder to ignore errors in real life. There are no erasers on our tongues. This leads to hurt and misunderstanding, especially if in the heat of conflict the act and the actor are lumped together and seen as one. I think it's possible to separate the deed from the doer; in fact, that is what forgiveness is all about. In chapter nine I explore the twin arts of being responsible for what we communicate and of being forgiving when communication goes awry. To promote responsibility and reconciliation at the same time is to shoot for human communication at its finest.

Communication = Content + Relationship.[10] I use this formula whenever I speak to a group about communication. It highlights the truth that what is said (content) is only part of an interpersonal transaction—a small part. The feeling that two people have for each other (relationship) dominates the flow of words. This is true in charades. Even a team of experts will be hopelessly inept if the players don't like each other. In chapter ten I make an unabashedly blatant pitch for greater intimacy in relationships.

At the risk of boring you, I tap into my reservoir of private truths concerning friendship. Maybe in the process I'll create some shared meaning. I think interpersonal closeness is the logical outcome of good communication. If strengthened friendship isn't the goal of a long-term relationship, why bother? So in the final chapter I cast off the garb of the neutral social scientist and put on the cloak of the passionate promoter of intimate bonds. I hope you're convinced.

The order of these chapters isn't random. I've set them up to cluster around the three kinds of understanding that can improve a one-on-one relationship. Suppose I desire to build a solid friendship with you. First, I must have a good grasp of who I am—*understanding me.* The chapters on self-concept and motivation focus on tools of self-awareness. Then I must apprehend who you are—*understanding thee.* The chapters on perception, listening to language, nonverbal communication and attraction aim at fostering that knowledge. Finally, I need to appreciate the personality of our

From the Wall Street Journal—Permission, Cartoon Features Syndicate

"It's not really all that important that we understand each other . . .
just that *you* understand *me.*"

relationship—*understanding we.* The idea of treating our bond as a living
entity may sound a bit strange, so let me elaborate.

When two people communicate, their relationship takes on a life of its
own. Some writers call this relationship a *spiritual child.*[11] The child springs
inevitably from the interaction, but that doesn't mean it's automatically
healthy. Its growth can be stunted by inattention and its well-being maimed
by ignorance or abuse. On the other hand, the "kid" can be nurtured by
high-quality communication. That's what the last three chapters are about.

They deal with topics such as trust, transparency, accountability, forgiveness and intimacy—the stuff of relational development.

Making friends isn't easy. There's no guarantee that interpersonal communication will produce intimacy. But without quality straight talk, lasting closeness is impossible. So let me encourage you to plunge into the process of understanding yourself, the other person and your relationship. It's hard work, but I hope you'll have fun along the way. We'll start with the self.

UNDERSTANDING ME

2
SELF-CONCEPT

Interpersonal communication
starts with the self.

WE WERE SITTING around the living room laughing at Bowser, our ridiculous bassett hound. "Look at that pitiful-looking beast," my daughter said. "It seems like God made him all wrong. His ears are too long, his legs are too short, and his skin is too big for his body. Poor Bowser."

"Aw, it doesn't bother him," my son piped in. "He doesn't even know he's alive."

My son was right: as far as we know, animals don't contemplate their own existence. But people do. God gave us the ability to get outside ourselves and ponder what we're like. This capacity isn't reserved for philosophers and heavy thinkers. We all have it. It's as if we have grandstand seats in the sky to watch ourselves play out our lives. What we see and conclude makes up our self-concept.

This chapter on self-concept will be quite personal. How could it be otherwise? We'll look at identity and self-esteem—two sides of self-concept. I'll discuss how we come to hold our particular self-definition, and how that image affects our relationships with other people. I'll conclude by suggesting ways we can change self-image—our own or someone else's.

Who Am I?

I'd like to ask you to take a systematic look at your self- concept. You can read about self-image until your eyes water, but the effort is wasted unless you come to grips with the image you hold of yourself. So pause for a few moments to take a blank piece of paper. At the top write, "Who am I?" Number down the side of the page from 1 to 15. After each number complete the sentence, "I am . . ." When you start, your paper will look like Table 1.

Now take a few minutes to write fifteen different responses. You're writing this for yourself—no one else will see it—so don't bother about what others might think of your answers. Also don't worry if your answers seem inconsistent or unimportant. Just put down whatever comes to mind. Try to finish in five to seven minutes. Do it now.

If you're like most folks, your list can be divided into two sets of items.[1] You used _nouns_ to describe various roles, positions and groups you see as yours. My list includes Christian, husband-father, Young Life leader, teacher, writer and pilot. These are discrete categories which tend to distinguish me from the human race as a whole. Not everyone in the world is a husband-father. By seeing parenthood as part of who I am, I've separated myself from well over fifty per cent of the population. Most fathers aren't teachers. Take away those who don't write and the pool becomes smaller. Although I wish it were otherwise, not all of this small group are Christians. When the requirements of being a Young Life leader and a pilot are added, the field is narrowed so drastically that only a handful of people in the world fit the description. In fact, I may be unique—the only one to see myself with this particular blend of roles, group loyalties and abilities. We can call this part of self-concept my _identity_.

You also used _adjectives_ to refer to personal attributes or personality

Who Am I?

I am:

1.

2.

3.

4.

5.

6.

7.

8.

9.

10.

11.

12.

13.

14.

15.

Table 1. A Self-Survey

traits you see within yourself. My list includes people-oriented, competitive, lazy, different, competent, supportive, manipulative. These terms are a bit more ambiguous than the nouns. They need some explanation. For instance, I see myself as competent—but in what area? Note also that some of these characteristics are positive, while others are negative or downright sinful. I'll fill you in on how I interpret these qualities.

People-oriented: I'm an extrovert. I like being with people. I don't think everyone should be this way, but I'm happy I am. (+)

Competitive: A contest stirs the juices within me. I love sports and games of all sorts. I did my best work in school when I was competing for a grade. Overall I like to win, but I realize that my competitiveness has the potential to get out of bounds and cause me to ride roughshod over others. (+?)

Lazy: I'm not disciplined. There's a bit of the mañana spirit within me. I like my creature comforts. I wish I weren't that way. (-)

Different: I like the idea that I don't follow the crowd. For 15 years I had a beard. Most of my colleagues were cleanshaven. As more grew beards, I decided to shave mine off. I like the name Em because it's different. (+)

Competent: I do well in a crisis. I can keep my cool. I'm intelligent and can usually pick up ideas quickly. I'm beginning to be a good mechanic. I'm thankful for these abilities. (+)

Manipulative: I have the tendency to use other people to gain what I want. I'm fairly skilled at it. I hate this part of me. I'm working hard to resist it. I think treating people as things is sin. (-)

Build others up: It makes me feel warm to see other people like themselves, to see them appreciate what God has made them. I believe that building others up is part of what God would have me do with my life. (+)

By now you're probably wondering what kind of strange bird this Em Griffin is. (Remember that what I've written is just my image of myself. Others may perceive me quite differently.) I've taken you through some of my responses to help you learn a good way to get in touch with your self-concept.

If you sum up the plusses and minuses on this partial list you'll get a fair idea of how I feel about myself. You can do the same with your survey.

This emotional or affective part of self-concept is usually called *self-esteem*.

You may find that not all your answers are easily coded in the categories of identity or self-esteem. However, since most responses fall into one of these two categories, we'll take a deeper look at them to see what they are and how they affect us.

Identity

Identity is the mind's-eye picture we have of ourselves. For some of us this is a crystal-clear image. We're in focus. We may not like all we see, but at least we know what's there. A well-focused identity is important for a couple of reasons.

© 1974 SR/Ward. Reprinted by permission of Orlando Busino.

"Of course you're going through an identity crisis—you're a chameleon."

In the first place, we all want to be special. It was with some satisfaction that I saw the flyer/Young Life leader/writer/father/teacher/Christian Em Griffin as possibly unique. If you doubt this panhuman desire to be different, try an experiment. Go up to a friend and announce boldly, "You're just like everyone else I know." Prepare to lose a friend. Some Christian fellowships place a strong emphasis on our sameness before God. These groups try to file off all the edges and corners that distinguish one believer from another. That's too bad. A great deal of comfort can come from realizing that Jesus knows my name and the number of hairs on my head—

and that the total count is different from anyone else's.

There's a second reason why a well-focused identity is an asset. We know what to expect from ourselves. Probably life's greatest frustration is uncertainty about the future. We can handle anything—good or bad—if we know for sure that it's coming. It's the not knowing that wears us down. As stated in chapter one, a main purpose of talking to others is to reduce that frustration. We communicate to bring order out of chaos—to make the future more predictable.

The nagging questions brought on by uncertainty about self have filled the pages of literature. The soldier in *The Red Badge of Courage* agonizes over whether or not he'll turn and run in the upcoming battle. James Dickey's *Deliverance* portrays a business executive taking to the wilderness because of self-doubts. He hopes to discover who he really is—to find out whether or not he'll have what it takes when faced with emergency. Most of Hemingway's characters vacillate until thrust into a "moment of truth." At this point they're hit with a bolt of self-enlightenment, and their pathway is set.

A clearly defined self-image can take a lot of the flux out of a situation. If we know what to expect from ourselves, that's one less variable to worry about. We can concentrate on other people's actions and external circumstances. We don't have to stew over our own response.

Unfortunately, a lot of folks have only a fuzzy picture of who they are. They see a blurred image. Their self-identity is murky. This is tragic, because it leads to a hesitant or fearful approach to the outside world. It's like the eighth-grade boy just entering puberty. Sometimes his voice sounds deep and resonant. Other times it cracks into a high squeak. The uncertainty devastates him. He usually ends up mumbling—and even that as seldom as possible.

There are certain periods in life when our identity is especially likely to blur. These are the times of major life change. The teen-age years are a case in point. The young high-school kid goes through dramatic bodily changes while at the same time trying to separate himself from his parents, adapt to new relationships and cope with the pressures of school. The "carefree days of youth" are mostly myth. Some societies provide elaborate rites of passage to help a kid get a handle on a new identity. We miss this in our Western culture. In America, the closest thing to a rite of passage is the driver's license exam. It's a rather flimsy reed for those who don't have a grasp of who they are. Many adolescents come through this period smelling like a rose, but it would be silly to downplay the difficulty. It's a tough time!

Other changes can cause a crisis of identity: marriage, the birth of a child, children leaving home, menopause, divorce, moving, death. I get anxious at just the thought of picking up and taking a different job in a new location. I recently received an offer of a teaching post with greater prestige at a higher salary. A number of factors went into my decision, but one reason I turned it down was the anticipated loss of identity. In Glen Ellyn, Illinois, I'm known. It's comforting to have people call me by name in the drug store, dry cleaner's and gas station. I've carved out a niche as a Young Life volunteer, hockey nut, communications teacher, Presbyterian layman and weekend pilot. I guess I'd rather be a big fish in a little pond than a little fish in a big pond. It's easier to have an identity in a little pond.

Stress, whether brought on by major life changes or by some other factor, can lead to self-alienation, a noxious feeling that comes from seeing our actions as foreign to our real selves. We see ourselves as kind, yet we do something cruel. We feel our life is a sham. In its extreme form, self-alienation can render a person psychotic—unable to cope with other people. Usually, however, it's a milder form of estrangement that makes us hesitant to act and slow to respond. A clear sense of identity is a prerequisite to bold action. The shakers and movers of this world are not always nice—sometimes they're downright mean. But they usually have a realistic image of who they are.

Suppose for a moment you walked into a room and stood before a full-length mirror. But instead of seeing your image reflected back to you, all you saw was the empty room. It would be as if you didn't exist. The experience would be shattering.

We are capable of shattering other people in this very way when we ignore them or are careless with them. Our thoughtless actions can rob them of their identity. I did this—to my shame—a few years ago.

I was in charge of a busload of kids going for a week to a Young Life camp. Since the thirty kids from my club didn't fill the bus, we also took four girls from a town thirty miles away. All during the week I spent time with "my kids" and the four other girls. We climbed mountains, rode horses, swam, ate, sang songs and read the Bible together. On the bus ride home I noticed an empty seat next to one of the four extra girls. Feeling a certain sense of duty for her well-being, I sat down next to her and asked in a friendly fashion if it had been a good week. I was bowled over by her response. She leveled me with a cold stare and stated, "You don't care." I assured her that I did—that I really hoped it had been great. She started to swear at me in a bitter voice. After a two-minute tirade she concluded, "You care so little about me that you can't even be bothered to remember my name." I started to protest until it hit me with a shock. She was right: I didn't know whether she was Sue, Sally, Peggy, or Joan. With deep embarrassment and remorse I asked her forgiveness. But it was too late. I had treated her as if she weren't there. I had wiped out her identity by not knowing her name.

Our identity is very much tied to our names. I was given the name Emory at birth. It was an odd name to most of the kids in school, and I got a lot of kidding about it. In eighth grade I was six feet tall but weighed only a bit over a hundred pounds. I was inordinately clumsy, and the kids would taunt me as I stumbled along. "Hey, there goes Emily," they'd yell in sarcastic voices. In high school, however, I became part of a group of guys and gals who liked me and gave me some recognition. They started calling me Em. To this day the name Em captures all the things I like about myself. It's the name on the cover of this book. Only a few special folks call me Emory.

It would be wrong to think of identity as fixed or rigid. There is no little carved stone statue of Em Griffin that is the "real me." All of us are in a constant state of flux. Whether we like it or not, change is the order of the day. Usually the alteration is a gradual and imperceptible process. Sometimes, however, identity change is sudden and dramatic.

Christ was talking about identity change when he told Nicodemus he must be born again. He needed to be completely made over so he would see the world and himself through different eyes. "If anyone is in Christ, he is a new creation; the old has gone, the new has come" (2 Cor 5:17). Jesus confirmed the radical change in Cephas by changing his name to Peter. In the same way Levi became Matthew.

A change in identity can bring about a change in actions. I became a Christian at a weekend camp my senior year of high school. No one sat down and prayed with me or told me I was in the kingdom. But I had a strong sense that I was a different person. At lunch on Monday I walked out of school with my brown bag lunch. I took out the usual apple and peanut-butter-and-jelly sandwich and then proceeded to crumple up the bag and throw it into a bush—as usual. After I had taken about four steps the thought hit me. "Wait a minute. I'm a Christian now. I can't do that anymore." So I retraced my steps, picked up the bag and carried it to a trash can a block away.

Actions affect identity too. There have been times in my Christian life when I've doubted whether God had any part in me. But then I think back to retrieving that crumpled sack and am reassured that I'm definitely in the faith.

There are a number of ways we can capture the key elements of our identity. The fifteen-item "Who Am I?" survey at the start of the chapter is one such effort. A second way is to observe our own behavior when we're thrust into crises.[2] How we react in a "moment of truth" is a pretty fair indication of what's in the inner core of our being. Peak experiences of danger, passion or grief are often the catalyst for self-discovery.

A third route to identity is to catalog the groups to which we belong.[3] It seems paradoxical, but one way we assert our individual uniqueness is by identifying with groups that take a public stand. It's almost impossible today to buy a sweatshirt that doesn't proclaim our allegiance to some school or school of thought. The Greek letters on a jacket, the logo on a baseball cap, the cross around the neck, the cards in our wallet—all of these announce who we are.

This approach wouldn't work for my wife, however. Jeanie's not a large-group person. This doesn't mean she lacks an identity. You'd merely have to spot it in a different way. Jeanie's an artist. Her warmth, sensitivity, contemplative nature, and desire for perfection come through in the way she paints on canvas or plays the piano. Jeanie's not alone. Many folks who avoid group affiliations express their identity in creative effort. This is a fourth method of coming to grips with identity. A work of art is a way of saying, "Here I am. This is me!"[4]

Self-Esteem

But identity is only half of the self-concept story. It's like a formal dictionary definition of an animal. It describes the beast, but not the response it arouses. There's no doubt that a puppy makes us feel warm inside but a crocodile scares us. Identity, like a definition, gives the denotation but not the connotation—the facts, not the feeling. We move into the crucial area of *self-esteem* when we ask how we feel about our mental self-portrait.

The question of self-esteem can be simply stated: Do I like myself? The answer is not always so simple. As you'll recall from my "Who Am I?" responses, I viewed myself with mixed emotions. I liked most of Em Griffin's qualities but was bothered by a few. My guess is that you feel the same way about yourself. The situation is further complicated by the fact that the total self-esteem package is divided into several parts. Usually the positive and negative attributes which come to mind shake down into four different slots or categories. Another way of putting this is that self-esteem is a firm wall made of four separate building blocks—each as important as the others.

The first building block is a *sense of moral worth*.[5] For people to have high self-esteem, they must be confident that they are approved by God—that they are basically okay. They need the inner assurance that they will react in a good or upright way when confronted with an ethical choice.

Two of my adjectives reveal my struggle in this area. I saw myself as manipulative and lazy. Since I first responded to that self-test I've discovered that sloth is part of my self-image. Every year my college presents an award for "Teacher of the Year." The winning name is kept a secret until the Dean makes the presentation at an awards convocation. It's an honor

I've always wanted. One year some faculty members told me they had nominated me. I thought I had a chance until the Dean started his presentation. He stated that the winner was hard-working and disciplined in his use of time. My immediate reaction was, "That leaves me out." As a matter of fact I received the prize—he was talking about me! But my gut response showed my negative self-image in this area.

The moral worth picture isn't entirely bleak for me, however. My negative view of myself as manipulative and lazy is tempered by my positive view that I am supportive—I am one who builds up others. I think God smiles and says, "Well done, my good and faithful servant," when I exercise this tendency. I'm glad I have this positive part. Because of Jesus Christ and his forgiveness, Christians are in a unique position to experience a sense of moral okayness. God has declared us worthwhile. Unfortunately, many in the church concentrate on their moral poverty and miss the joy of this assurance. More of this later.

Building block number two is _a sense of competence._ I even used the term _competent_ in my response to the fifteen-item survey. Of course, this doesn't mean I consider myself a jack-of-all-trades. If I felt I had to be an expert in everything, I'd be doomed to have a bum self-image for life. As one of my colleagues puts it, "We're all laymen in every area save one." Instead I'm selective. I feel pretty good about my ability to teach, speak, fly a plane, swim and work with teen-agers.

Notice that this feeling of competence is only partially determined by my actual ability. The other factor is the height of my expectation. You might find it helpful to think of this in terms of the following formula:[6]

$$\text{SELF-ESTEEM} = \frac{\text{SUCCESS (actual ability)}}{\text{HOPES (expectation)}}$$

My self-esteem will rise if I either increase my skill or scale down my pretensions. Of course the reverse is also true. I'll become discouraged if expectations rise without an equal rise in competence. I've seen this happen in my family. Jeanie works extremely hard at her paintings, and over the years there has been a dramatic increase in quality that's plain for all to see. As one who can't draw a straight line with a ruler, I'm astounded at what she can do with a brush. But while her ability has grown, so have her expectations. She's her most severe critic.

You'll recall that I described myself as "different." This term illustrates the third building block of self-esteem—*a sense of self-determination*. When I was in high school I had to memorize a poem by William Henley. Two lines have stuck with me: "I am the master of my fate;/I am the captain of my soul." Even before I became a Christian I thought this was a rather arrogant claim. But at the same time I'm intrigued by the idea that I could have control over my destiny. I've since learned that a feeling of self-determination is crucial for a positive self-concept.

"Send the paranoids in first—the ones with inferiority complexes don't mind waiting."

Folks who have a low view of themselves usually feel powerless to change their lives. They see themselves as a cork bobbing on a wave, a cloud driven by the wind, a pawn in the game of life. Conversely, men and women with positive self-regard are willing to accept responsibility for their own lives. They feel like subjects rather than objects, actors as opposed to those who are acted upon.

The final brick in the structure of self-esteem is *a sense of unity*. This may sound vague and hard to get a handle on, but I mean something quite specific. A sense of unity means that my right hand knows what my left hand is doing. My behavior is consistent over time. I'm not always wondering, "Now, why in the world did I do that?" The idea of integration or unity is well captured in the phrase "having it all together."

I said I was people-oriented. Throughout my life I can see a consistent stream of feelings, beliefs and actions centering around my desire to enjoy and work with others. A hermit I am not. The same sense of unity is obvious in my competitiveness. Just in the last day I competed in the following ways:

☐ sprained an ankle playing in a two-hour soccer game

☐ got caught up in a four-man game of darts

☐ tried to write a test which would have more validity than the one I wrote last week

☐ waxed a floor with a friend and was quite conscious of trying to get my half looking better than his side

☐ competed with myself to write more on this chapter today than I did yesterday

Now, you may be scratching your head and wondering how I can be fiercely competitive and a people person at the same time. If I felt these two characteristics were dissonant, it would certainly affect my self-esteem. So far, however, I've been able to reconcile the two in my own mind, seeing them as two parts of the same consistent Em Griffin package. It may be sheer rationalization, but this sense of all-togetherness is necessary if I'm going to feel good about myself.

Let's review for a second. Our self-concept is made up of our identity—the picture we have of ourselves, plus our self-esteem—how we feel about the images in that picture. I've talked about a positive self-esteem as a firm wall which we can lean against. The wall has four building blocks: a sense of moral worth, a sense of competence, a sense of self- determination, and a sense of unity. The larger the bricks, the higher and more solid our internal support—or to put it more bluntly, the more we like ourselves. Now the big question is this: What difference does self-appreciation make in the way we act around others? If self-esteem doesn't have any noticeable effect on behavior, it's ridiculous to waste time talking about it.

What's the Difference?
A lot of wild claims for self-esteem have been bandied about in recent years. Some authors would have you believe that those who like themselves are some kind of psychic superhumans. Depending on what you read, a positive mental attitude will make you into a supersalesman, a magnetic leader of the masses, a sexual Don Juan, a one hundred per cent empathetic counselor, or a spiritual giant. Many of these supposed advantages are exaggerated, and a few are downright silly. But there are well-documented effects of high self-esteem which seem to give a person a head start in his dealings with others. I'll list four.

1. People who like themselves tend to talk more freely in groups.[7] In fact, you could probably take a stopwatch and clipboard to a group discussion and figure out which folks have high self-regard just by keeping track of how often and how long each one speaks. People who like themselves will participate. People who don't will hold back.

I was an exception to this rule. My nickname in junior high was "The Mouth." Not a very flattering way to be known, but it was an apt description of my behavior. No matter where I was or whom I was with, I would talk. This didn't spring from a high self-image, but rather from a desperate need for attention. At the time, I was a real klutz at sports, didn't get good grades and had few friends. I felt I had nothing in my repertoire that would cause others to notice me. But I discovered that by talking loud and long, I could force people to pay me grudging attention. Hence the prophetic nickname for one who later was to become a communications teacher. But don't let the glaring exceptions cause you to lose sight of the rule. Self-doubt usually causes silence and withdrawal. Self-liking leads to participation.

2. People who have a good self-image tend to be more spontaneous than those who are down on themselves.[8] They have an "I'll try anything once" approach to life. People who like themselves seem to be turned on by potential rewards and are willing to take risks to get them, while folks who see themselves as low on the totem pole are motivated much more by possible costs or losses.[9] Their aim is to preserve what corner of themselves they like rather than to boldly strike out to become fuller persons. Therefore they're hesitant in their dealings with others. They aren't even sure they can count on themselves.

IN A QUANDARY

Drawing by R. Chast; © 1983 The New Yorker Magazine, Inc.

Spontaneity is a fun quality to watch. I once worked with a high-school kid who had it in spades. Dave's mother made him wear mukluk boots to school in the winter so his feet wouldn't get wet. Now most teen-agers in our town wouldn't be caught dead in galoshes, and they'd die in a pile if their friends found out they were wearing them on mother's orders. But Dave was so unself-conscious that he not only wore the silly-looking things, but joked about how easily he gave in to his mother's desires. Needless to say, Dave was quite comfortable with who he was.

Self-confidence is not static. It can rise and fall like the Dow Jones stock-market index. At different times one can be either bullish (+) or bearish (-) toward oneself. One researcher manipulated college men's self-esteem in the laboratory in order to determine the effect of self-esteem on risk taking.[10] In the morning session he gave fake test scores to all participants. Some fellows were told they were intelligent, motivated and personable. Others received the bad news that they scored quite low in these qualities.

The experimenter then called for an hour's lunch break. There was a reason for this. He had arranged for an extremely attractive girl, who was supposedly a subject in another experiment, to be free at exactly the same time. Would a guy take a chance and ask the girl to join him for lunch, or would he spend the hour alone? The researcher guessed that self-esteem would make the difference.

It did. He found that men who had their image buoyed up usually took the plunge and asked the girl to join them. However, those whose self-confidence had been shaken weren't willing to face the possibility of being turned down. They ate lunch by themselves.

3. People with low self-regard are usually easier to sway.[11] Having a low opinion of their attitudes and actions, they are prime candidates for something better. Earlier I mentioned that the teen-age years (and teen-age self-image) are full of flux. This renders the teen-ager quite susceptible to influence—not only to music fads and the claims of pimple medication, but to matters of faith as well. Groups like Young Life and Youth for Christ are effective because they address an age group that's open to change.

High-school students don't have a corner on the low self-image market. The downtrodden of all ages make the easiest converts. Mass movements have traditionally been fueled with people who feel they have little to lose. Paul notes that the early church wasn't peopled with many winners. Few of Christ's followers were wise as the world judges wisdom; not many were powerful, and only a smattering were of noble birth. Most were weak, low and despised (1 Cor 1:26-29).

Hypnosis provides another example of this linkage. Not everyone can be put into a trance. People with a weak self-image are more likely to respond to hypnotic suggestion.

So we see that there's a high correlation between self-esteem and persuasibility. People who feel good about themselves resist change. They usually like the way their life is going, so they want to maintain the status quo. They find it easy to shrug off group pressure or ignore a persuasive appeal. But as self-doubt increases, so does the force of outside argument and the impact of others' ideas.

There's a flip side to this. People with high self-esteem make more persuasive attempts than folks with a low self-image.[12] If you are plagued with self-doubts you usually won't bother trying to convince others to adopt your beliefs or behavior. Self-esteem and assertiveness are linked.

4. The world looks pretty good to those with lots of self- esteem.[13] Life seems basically positive. In their dealings with other people, folks with a good self-image tend to bear all things, believe all things, hope all things, endure all things (1 Cor 13:7). Please don't jump to conclusions. You don't have to be a Pollyanna or the proud owner of rose-colored glasses to like yourself. But thinking you're okay and liking the world around you seem to go together.

On the other hand, some people view life as basically hostile. It's a jungle out there. I'm reminded of Eeyore, the donkey, in the stories of Winnie the Pooh. Eeyore is relentlessly negative. He walks around with a perpetual cloud of gloom hanging over his head. No matter how well things are going for the moment, he knows everything will turn out lousy in the end. Not surprisingly, Eeyore has a real problem with self-image.

I recently ran across a statement which sums up the linkage between self-image and attitude toward others. John Claypool, a successful and sensitive pastor, had hoped his decision to become a minister would please his mother. "But she was not the kind of person that could ever give that kind of blessing," he said, "because she never did like herself, and therefore she had trouble ever liking the way anything was."[14]

It's hard to say which comes first—a low self-image or a poor world view. Although they probably feed on each other, my guess is that poor self-esteem is more often the cause than the effect. When we feel bum about ourselves we adjust our world to match the mood.

There's an interesting sidelight to the whole positive-negative question. Folks with high self-esteem can handle criticism better than those who are down on themselves.[15] Let's face it, nobody really likes criticism. But people with a good dollop of self-confidence can benefit from constructive suggestions. They sift the words for possible help in doing a better job. They even get impatient with endless praise or empty flattery. They're looking for an honest, expert evaluation and are willing to take their lumps to get it. Criticism is tougher on those who question their self-worth. They feel "dumped on" and quickly become defensive.

Is All This Christian?

"Wait a minute, Em. All this talk about the advantages of a good self-image is too much. You make it sound as though having high personal regard is akin to possessing a pearl of great price—just short of finding the Holy Grail. You've painted a picture of self-esteem as a virtue. But Paul warns against those who are proud, arrogant, swollen with conceit, lovers of self (2 Tim 3:2-5). Isn't self-appreciation a sin?"

I'm tempted just to write no and move on. I get impatient with the purveyors of worm theology. They would have us believe that people are without a shred of decency. If they had their way, these Christians would mope around in sackcloth and ashes, mumbling, "I am nothing, I am worthless." But an angry retort doesn't do justice to the nagging fears of many that there is something suspect about liking yourself.

Let's start with creation. When God created the world he said it was good. The sun, the moon, the sea, the land, the fish, the animals—all were judged good. When God created man and woman he said they were very good. Not just okay or passable—very good. If God sees us as very good, should we see ourselves as less?

But of course there's the Fall. Doesn't disobedience render us worthless? No. Despite our sin, God still thinks we are worth redeeming. It's a mistake to think the Fall wiped out the effectiveness of God's creation. Rather, it set the stage for redemption. Not only are human beings worthwhile for what they can be; they are precious for what they are right now.

Let me put it another way. We often speak as though we became valuable when Christ died for us. But that's wrong. Christ's death revealed the tremendous value God already placed on us. Jesus saved us because we were worth saving.

When a scribe asked Jesus to state the greatest commandment, our Lord named two. The second was to love our neighbor as ourselves (Mark 12:30). That's a rather strong mandate for self-appreciation. Now, I suppose someone could object: "Wait. Jesus isn't advocating self-love. He's merely recognizing our selfishness and using it as a point of comparison."

But this doesn't do justice to Christ's words. In the two commandments he outlines a love trilogy which is intertwined: Love God; love others; love self.

Self-love is to be realistic. In Romans, Paul argues for an honest self-appraisal: "I say to every one of you: Do not think of yourself more highly than you ought, but rather think of yourself with sober judgment, in accordance with the measure of faith God has given you" (Rom 12:3). The purpose of this self-love is to free us from preoccupation with self so that we can concentrate on others. As he puts it later in the chapter, we are to prefer one another, outdoing "one another in showing honor" (v. 10 RSV). We err when we imagine that humility means self-abasement. Paul says, "Do nothing out of selfish ambition or vain conceit, but in humility consider others better than yourselves" (Phil 2:3). Humility doesn't mean knocking ourselves down. It means building others up.

So two possible attitudes toward self emerge from Scripture. One is *selfishness.* In this greedy kind of parasitic love, others are swallowed up by a bottomless pit. They are served—on a plate—to gratify an insatiable appetite for self-glory. Selfishness is sin.

The other attitude toward self is *self-love.* It's the attitude Christians should have—loving themselves and loving others. If we begin to hate ourselves, we will start to hate others too. How could it be otherwise? We can't resign from the human race. The less we think of ourselves, the less we will think of other human beings as well.

This is tough for many Christians to grasp. They've focused on their sinfulness so long that self-appreciation seems immoral. This year I led a weekend retreat for unmarried young adults in their twenties and thirties. This group is low in society's pecking order to begin with. Former friends are married. Parents ask some not-so-subtle questions. The fact that they are Christians doesn't help much. Most churches have no programs geared to their needs. One fellow deprecatingly referred to the group as the "Young Hornies."

I got them together in small groups and asked them to share some things they liked about themselves. Personality traits, attitudes, awards, accomplishments—anything was fair game. It was rugged. A few simply wouldn't—

Reprinted with permission from *Leadership*.

"How did the singles group respond to your suggestion
that they call themselves 'The Leftovers'?"

or couldn't—do it. But those who haltingly voiced some hidden thoughts of self-worth felt a tremendous sense of relief. As one man put it, "I've sung 'Jesus Loves Me' since I was a kid, but I've only believed it in my head. For the first time, I feel like I might be truly lovable."

God loves us. He wants us to join him.

"Okay," you say. "I'm convinced. It's vitally important that I have a sense of moral worth, competence, togetherness and self- determination. I know I'll be more active, spontaneous, persuasive and positive in my dealings with others if I do. I believe that God is pleased when I have a positive self-concept. But I'm just not that confident. I continually get down on myself. In fact, I'm my own worst critic. How can I improve my self-image?"

Ah, there's the rub. Self-esteem doesn't change easily. Part of me wishes I could include magic pixie dust with each copy of this book. You could read this chapter and sprinkle on the powder, and your self-regard would go up seven notches. I'd use the stuff myself. But I'm fresh out of pixie dust. And God didn't set up the world that way. Self-image is shaped over a lifetime and yields to change very slowly. Let's take a brief look at how it's formed.

The Looking-Glass Self

Emerson wrote:

Each to each a looking glass
Reflects the other that doth pass.

We judge our worth by looking into mirrors. Not objective reflectors that hang on walls, but moving mirrors that can be kind or cruel. These mirrors are the people we're with every day.

We form our self-images by seeing ourselves through the eyes of other people.[16] We take the role of another person—pretending for an instant that we are he—and view ourselves from his perspective. This phenomenon is known as the "Looking-Glass Self."

It starts early. As infants in cribs we looked to our parents for hints about ourselves. When they smiled down at us, our world was good and so were we. If they frowned or used a harsh tone, the world became lousy and we felt bad about ourselves. We may sometimes wonder if psychologists make too much of the importance of early childhood influences. Yet the evidence won't go away. A good self-regard, or a poor one, develops in a child's first few years. It's hard to shake those early feelings.

Suppose you're three years old and a friend of your mother offers you a choice of lollipops—either green or red. You have no strong preference for lime or cherry, and you let her know you don't care. Your baby sister reaches for the red one, so your mom's friend hands you the lime. Note that your behavior can be interpreted two different ways. Your mom may turn to her friend and say, "Johnny's such a fine boy. He's really flexible. I wish Suzy weren't so grabby." Or she could react less favorably. "John's such a wishy-washy child. He can never make up his mind." Your action is the same in either case. But the label your parent attaches to it makes a huge difference in your self-esteem.

The process continues into adulthood. Others attribute meaning to our lives. They see us as either

flexible or wishy-washy

firm or stubborn

courageous or foolhardy

sensible or chicken

generous or wasteful

thrifty or tight-fisted

enthusiastic or unstable

steady or dull

They bounce back their reactions, and our self-esteem goes up or down accordingly. Reality has little to do with it. What counts is the interpretation others place upon our behavior.

This fact of life is dramatized in George Bernard Shaw's play *Pygmalion* and its Broadway adaptation, *My Fair Lady*. Eliza Doolittle is a common flower vendor in the street. Professor Henry Higgins takes her under his wing and teaches her to speak and act like a proper British lady. He ultimately passes her off in high society as a princess. Higgins attributes this success to the change he has engineered in her speech. Not so, according to Eliza. When she left the London gutter, people changed their expectations of her. As she elegantly states it at the end of the play: "The difference between a flower girl and a lady is not how she acts; it's how she's treated."[17]

Do unto Others
One implication of the looking-glass self is evident. I see no alternative for Christians: if we really care about other people, we'll build them up. It's also a great way to make friends.

Of course a simple compliment isn't going to bring about a great change in a friend's self-regard. He may be fighting a lifetime of put-downs. It's ridiculous to think that one positive word will turn the tide of consistent self-depreciation. Our encouragement may be discounted. It may even go unheard. But we have to start somewhere.

Perhaps the first hurdle to clear is to convince people that change is possible. We are in process. We haven't arrived yet. We are becoming. The idea of change is part of American tradition. A sign in an Old West saloon captured this value:

I ain't what I ought to be
I ain't what I could be
But I ain't what I was.[18]

We need to help others see that change is a legitimate option.

Then we must systematically set out to affirm them. Does this sound calculated? I hope so. I'm convinced that ego alteration doesn't happen by accident. I have a poster in my office that pictures an old-time gumball machine which has just spilled out about a dozen gumballs gratis. The caption reads, "I suspect someone of plotting to make me happy." Start plotting.

Jeanie has helped me in this. When our kids were young she decided to praise them consistently. She also hooked me into the plan. At first I was worried that they'd get swollen heads. But Jeanie was adamant. "Look, they're going to get knocked down by teachers, friends and the world at large. There ought to be one safe haven for them where they can relax and get bathed in affirmation. As for me and my household, we will build them up." She convinced me. I've become even more persuaded as I've watched the effects on Jim and Sharon. I even suspect Jeanie of adopting the same tactics toward me. It's been great.

Can the church be this sort of haven? I think so. Christians can love, because God first loved us (1 Jn 4:19). We've experienced *agape* love—love not because we are particularly lovely, but because we desperately need it. Therefore we should be equipped to reach out in love to others. Apparently this was the case in the early church. Acts 2 paints a picture of a supportive, affirming body. The heathen world looked on and said, "See how they love one another."

But even among Christians we have to work at giving positive strokes. It doesn't come naturally. I experimented the other day with spectacular results. I was on a high-school retreat with a fourteen-year-old fellow named Steve. As we were walking together toward the cabin it struck me that he was a handsome guy. Ordinarily, I wouldn't have said anything. It's not the kind of thing one guy says to another. But I decided to let him in on my reaction. I turned and said, "You know, Steve, you're a good-looking guy." He stopped and looked at me in wonder. "You're kidding, Em." I assured him I meant what I said. It turned out no one had ever told him that before. If it was really true, he asked, how come all his friends joked about his appearance? This led to a short discussion on our natural insecurities and how they lead to sarcasm. As we reached the cabin he said, "I'll bet it was fun for you to make me feel good. Sometime today I'll let Eric know he's a really neat guy." Not bad for a ninth-grade kid.

I realize compliments can be forced or foolish, but don't get scared off by the dangers or abuses of affirmation. Be patient. Wait until you catch people in the act of doing something you genuinely appreciate. Then let them know. If we fail to give these positive strokes to others, the results can be tragic. You probably know a number of people who match this description: "It is the person most deficient in self-esteem who exerts himself to get it. Most touching is the individual so lacking the love or affection of others that his grasping demands stifle precisely those who might be able to fulfill his needs."[19]

This seems to fit with Jesus' puzzling statement, "To everyone who has, more will be given, but as for the one who has nothing, even what he has will be taken away" (Lk 19:26).

This section was fun to write. *Build others up* is a simple prescription and I know it works. But what can you do if the problem is yours, not someone else's? It's not quite so easy to suggest ways to build up your own self-esteem. Don't quit reading, however. The final section of this chapter contains a mixture of ideas culled from research, observation and my own struggles with self-esteem.

Do unto Yourself

None of the following suggestions are guaranteed, you-betcha, sure-fire winners. But they're better than moping around feeling sorry for yourself. Introspection is a killer. The more you worry about your self-image, the lower it will go.[20] That's why we usually cringe when we hear our voices on a tape recorder, or groan when we see a candid photograph—they make us self-conscious. Perhaps I've done you a disservice by even raising the idea of self-concept. If so, I apologize. It was a calculated risk. But if you're stewing about how crummy you are, experiment with these suggestions.

1. *Toss yourself into a meaningful cause.* This is a time-tested remedy for combating low self-esteem. Christians have an advantage in overcoming self-despair. We have a Lord who invites us to plunge into his cause—the Kingdom of God. Perhaps this is an added meaning of Christ's statement, "Whoever who loses his life for my sake will find it" (Mt 10:39).

A worthwhile goal doesn't have to be grand and glorious. Training hard for the big football game, collecting signatures on a petition against environmental pollution, helping your buddies in the army, sacrificing to get the kids through college, processing a special rush order on the job—all these can help us turn our eyes outward. When the cause is important enough to make us forget ourselves and concentrate on the common good, our self-esteem will improve. Even if we fail, it makes little difference. It's the quest itself, not the result, that counters nagging self-consciousness.

2. *Surround yourself with folks who make you feel good.* Does it seem that some people have deliberately set out to tear you down? Every time you begin to like yourself a bit, they clobber you over the head with some new failure or dump a fresh load of guilt on you. Who needs it? Of course you can try to change them, to get them to be more affirming. (Good luck.) Or you can quietly take your leave and seek a more supportive environment. This may mean a radical shift. In severe cases, leaving an old circle of "friends," changing jobs or staying away from destructive relatives may be the only solution.

3. *Share your feelings with someone else.* We often have tunnel vision: we think we invented sin and everyone else is perfect. Or we know we have great gobs of self-doubt, and we think others have life well in hand. It's natural to assume that others look down on us for our lack of excellence. But all sorts of good things can happen when we bring these thoughts to the surface:

☐ We find out that our mind-reading skill is faulty. The other person really likes us and thinks we're great.

☐ We discover that this paragon of virtue and ability is plagued by the same questions of worth that trouble us. While we don't want to wallow together in some slough of despond, it's comforting to know we aren't alone.

☐ We get a new perspective on our problem. The junk in our lives may not look quite so shabby in the light of day.

4. *Seek professional counseling.* This is a follow-up to the previous suggestion. Sometimes it's hard to find a sympathetic ear, a friend sensitive enough to respond in a helpful way. It's also possible that our low self-esteem is so deeply rooted in our personality that it will take more than a Band-Aid to close the wound. A trained psychologist, psychiatrist or

pastoral counselor could start the healing process.

Many Christians are leery of counseling. They believe a deep emotional need reflects a lack of spiritual maturity. If they could somehow get into a right relationship with God, they think, everything would be fine. This is overly optimistic. We're often victims of someone else's sin. We may not be able to pull ourselves up by our spiritual bootstraps. It's the height of vanity to assume that a good devotional life will clear up self-hate. God can use a counselor to heal, just as he uses a doctor to set a broken bone. I speak as one who has received great help from professional counseling. If you're hurting bad, don't sell the idea of professional counseling short.

5. *Don't take yourself too seriously.* Be willing to laugh at yourself. Let's face it: we do a lot of ridiculous things every day. There are two possible reactions to these failures. We can go the Pharisee route—cover up our mistakes and proceed through life with grim determination. Or we can openly chuckle at our ineptness and try again. The second alternative is much easier on our self-esteem.

Christians can be a pretty humorless bunch. We often treat every situation as a spiritual battleground. That's unfortunate. I'm utterly convinced that God wants us to take him seriously—but not ourselves. Willingness to laugh is one way to overcome anxiety. Humor is a great tension release. You don't have to be a comedian to take advantage of it—just think about the day's happenings so far, and you'll find plenty to laugh about. When your self-esteem isn't at stake at every turn, you'll be able to relax more. Fortunately, God doesn't require us to constantly prove ourselves.

6. *Change the way you look.* Self-esteem is tightly coupled with our body image.[21] It's hard to like yourself if you don't like the way you look. We can easily deplore the world's fanatical pursuit of physical beauty. Our society has obviously gone overboard. But it is equally wrong to dismiss the importance of the body. It's more than the container or outer shell. Scripture makes it clear that my body is an integral part of who I am.

Some Christians think it's wrong to change the body God gave them. Even the desire to do so is suspect. Passive acceptance is the rule. "What you see is what you get." I disagree. I've seen giant leaps of self-liking come from changes in appearance. Some examples:

☐ the adolescent girl who lost thirty pounds.

☐ the teen-aged boy who went to the dermatologist to control a severe case of acne.

☐ the seminary student who had a plastic surgeon alter his ears, which stuck out like Mickey Mouse's.

☐ the woman who had reconstructive surgery following the trauma of breast cancer.

☐ the retired minister who exercised his body into shape for the first time in his life.

Obviously there must be balance here. It's self-defeating to become preoccupied with looks. But if you comb your hair, shave or cut your fingernails for the sake of appearance, you might also consider other alterations. If you don't like what you see when you look in a mirror, ask yourself seriously what you might do to change.

7. *Practice assertiveness.* My self-esteem hit rock bottom fifteen years ago when I walked out of a new car showroom, having been badgered and bullied into paying list price for a car I wasn't even sure I wanted. I felt like a doormat. I resolved then and there that it would be different the next time. A few years later I devised a strategy for car buying and role-played it with a friend. He pretended to be the pushy salesman; I was the buyer. He tried all sorts of ploys on me, and I attempted to counter them. Although I started out rather tentative and uncertain, I was loaded for bear by the time I was ready to buy. I don't know if I got bottom price on the car, but I sure felt better than I had the previous time.

Assertiveness training is a role-playing technique. It gives you a chance to work through tough interpersonal dilemmas before they come up. You gain confidence that you won't be steamrollered into something against your will. A lot of folks don't need this kind of help. In fact, some of us are too inflexible as it is. But if you tend to be timid and acquiesce when someone comes on strong, play-acting practice will firm up your backbone for actual encounters with snippy sales clerks, aluminum siding phonies, or associates who always have to be right. One or two successes can do wonders for flagging self-respect.

8. *Know thyself.* Greater self-understanding usually leads to increased

comfort with who we are. It also improves our one-on-one communication. That's why I've scattered a number of self-scoring personality measures throughout this book, and why I've devoted chapters two and three to "Understanding Me." I often hear folks reflect on something they've said and wonder aloud, "Why did I say that?" The next chapter on motivation tries to answer that puzzled query. When we understand the *whys* of our behavior, the *whats* seem to fall into place.

3
MOTIVATION

The chances for effective communication increase as people become aware of their motives for getting together.

I USED THE TERM *competitive* to describe myself in the "Who Am I?" survey in the last chapter. This wasn't a new thought for me. I've had a growing realization that one of my primary motivations is an unquenchable drive to win. Like the old fire-station horse responding to the bell, I can feel my juices start to flow when I'm placed in a win/lose situation.

Does this self-understanding dampen my urge to compete? Not really. Motives change slowly, if at all. I'm still competitive—but understanding my motivation gives me power. I no longer have to be a one-trick pony under the sway of unrecognized drives. Realizing my tendency, I gain new options. I can choose to throw myself into the competitive fray as always, or I can choose to resist that impulse and act differently. I am still drawn to competitive situations, but I am no longer driven. That flexibility feels nice.

All of us are drawn toward other people—we all have social needs. Few of us, however, know *why* we want to get together with others. If we don't understand our motivations, we limit our options. We don't have the freedom to choose our responses. Because I think others share my quest for understanding what draws us toward other people, I'll first discuss the social motivations that stir people. Then I'll present some tools for discovering which motivations dominate our lives.

There's a danger here. It would be possible to use this material to psych others out in a type of motivational parlor game that leaves us cynical about our fellow human beings. But I'm not presenting this information to be used on others. As Jesus reminded us, we need to look for things that cloud our own vision, not concentrate on our brother's internal state. The truth we discover about our own motivations can set us free from unthinking, knee-jerk responses.

The Meaning of Motivation

Let's start by acknowledging that we share certain physiological needs with our pet dog or cat. We all want to quench thirst, satisfy our rumbling stomachs, sleep on a somewhat regular basis and avoid being poked with sharp sticks.[1] We also feel at least periodic spasms of sexual desire. But with the notable exception of the sexual urge, these creature drives are relatively uninteresting when we're trying to understand why we do what we do. We need to identify what's uniquely human and what makes humans differ from each other.

Our true colors often emerge when we're under extreme stress. Whether it's the young army recruit in his first exchange of gunfire, the business executive on an Outward Bound wilderness trek, the college girl studying for comprehensive exams or the housewife taking her first skydive, these peak experiences provide a rich source of motivational knowledge.

Viktor Frankl, a Jewish psychiatrist caught up in Hitler's holocaust, was sent to Auschwitz—but unlike ninety-five per cent of the inmates, he didn't die. Frankl discovered a common thread among the few survivors: they all had a reason and a fierce desire to live. For Frankl, it was the determination to publish his research. For others, it was the dream of reunion with loved ones. For still others, it was the white heat of revenge. They endured the horrible conditions of prison camp so that one day they could reverse

ED THRAXTON, JR.   A SELF-STARTER

the captor-victim roles. Frankl concluded that the will to meaning is what makes us human.[2] We have an irrepressible need to make our lives significant, make sense, have purpose.

As a Christian, I believe God has built into us the need for meaning, and this gnawing desire is satisfied only in relationship to him. But whether or not we credit God as the source of this longing, the will to meaning is the best overall explanation for our everyday behavior. Motives are the wellsprings of action, and once we've passed the threshold of bare survival, our ultimate motive is to give meaning to our short time on earth.

This meaning comes in three ways. We can find it by accomplishing worthwhile tasks, by developing satisfying relationships or by exercising an impact on another's life. We are motivated to do these things by our need for achievement, our need for affiliation and our need for power.[3]

The Need for Achievement

The need for achievement—often abbreviated *nAch*—is the desire to meet a self-imposed standard of excellence. A friend named Bruce comes immediately to mind. He started out selling popcorn at basketball games and is now worth millions as a real estate developer. I introduced him to another friend, and the conversation went like this:

Friend: Nice to meet you. What's your business?

Bruce: I buy low, sell high.

Friend: What product?

Bruce: What difference?

To Bruce, the deal is everything. He claims money isn't important; it's just a way of keeping score. He says he'd play just as hard for jelly beans. I believe him. Don't get the idea that Bruce is a cold calculating machine. He's a caring person who reaches out to others daily. But as one who gets his jollies from winning the game, Bruce is the archetypal high-nAch person.

We aren't all like Bruce, but many of us share his drive to succeed. The person for whom achievement is paramount might describe it this way: "I am a goal-oriented person. It's important to me to complete a job I've started. For that reason I try not to waste time. I have a strong desire to do things better, to constantly improve my performance."[4]

The Need for Affiliation

"People who need people are the luckiest people in the world." If what Barbara Streisand sings is true, we're all lucky. We humans all need to give and receive love. Even a hermit often lavishes affection on an animal.

The person high in need of affiliation (nAff) could say, "I am a role-oriented person. I'm very aware of what others are feeling, and I have strong emotional responses myself. It's important to me that people get along with and enjoy other people. I don't want to be left out."

I think of a friend named Melinda. Her life gains special meaning through quality relationships. As an undergrad she zoomed off the scale in her desire for intimacy, self-disclosure and interpersonal harmony. Now she's working on a masters degree in counseling.

Does that make Melinda a better Christian than Bruce? Not at all. They both seek to make their lives meaningful for God. But Bruce's natural inclination is to do it through production; Melinda's, through relationships. I admire them both.

The Need for Power
Power is a dirty word to most people. That's unfortunate. The need to have

an impact on others (nPow) is just as worthy as the need for achievement or affiliation. The best pastors often have a high need for power.

Of course, like the other two needs, the need for power can either be satisfied selfishly or channeled to make God's world more pleasing to him. Bruce could close deals and then hoard the profits, but he doesn't. Melinda could squeeze others dry for her own gratification without giving to them, but she doesn't. Likewise John could use his power to make others jump through hoops—but he doesn't.

John is a pastor who wants to influence others. If he weren't in the ministry, he'd be in politics. He loves to speak to groups and is good at friendly, one-on-one persuasion. He understands Lincoln's adage that you catch more bees with a teaspoon of honey than with a bucket of spit. John takes great satisfaction in helping people open their lives to God. He feels similar pleasure in guiding people down the path of social justice. He could express his need for power in the following words: "I am an effect-oriented person. I want to change the world. I'm not sidetracked by petty circumstances in my quest to have an impact on people. I have a strong desire to use my abilities to persuade others."

Make no mistake. For all of us our first impulse is survival. Give a man a virile case of stomach flu, and for the next twenty-four hours he won't think much about metaphysical meaning. But once he's reasonably confident he'll see tomorrow, his intrinsic need to give life meaning will resurface. That fulfillment can come through achievement, affiliation or power.

Is it possible to be stimulated by more than one of these desires? Yes. Some feel the force of all three motives. But in most people one is stronger than the other two, and this gives a peculiar cast to their lives.

Think of the Gospel writers. They describe the same Jesus, but each of them views Christ through his own motivational glasses.

Matthew, the businessman, sees a Jesus who accomplishes much. He comes to fulfill the Law, and Matthew interprets his every action in light of Old Testament promises. At every step of the way, Jesus achieves his goals and meets the standard of excellence.

John pictures the same God/man in terms of relationships. Love, friendship, commitment and human ties impress this evangelist.

Mark presents a Jesus of power and action. His words have authority, the wind and waves obey him, his omnipotence constantly leaks out.

Three writers, each viewing the world according to his own motivations.

Identifying your Motivational Make-Up

I'm writing this chapter while on leave from my teaching job at Wheaton College. I'm also using some of the time to test a variety of ultralight airplanes. Critics of ultralights describe them as glorified lawn chairs with bed-sheet wings pushed into the air by snowmobile engines.

Some people think I'm crazy. As one colleague stated, "You haven't taken a leave of absence. You've taken a leave of your senses. Do you have some kind of death wish? Why in the world do you want to go up in those contraptions?"

Why questions are never easy to answer. The most obvious way to identify my motivation is through introspection. After all, who is better equipped than I to spot what makes me tick? My guess is you've already matched yourself against the three descriptions I gave and have decided which motivation is "up" in your life.

One caution, however: we who are sinful are capable of great amounts of self-deception. I might conclude the reason I want to fly a two-seat ultralight is to share the fun with friends (nAff), while it's possible my real desire is to scare them out of their wits (nPow).

I think of women who selected a particular cake of soap in a consumer test.[5] When asked why they picked that brand, they invariably talked about its cleansing properties, scent and low price. But a videotape of the selection process showed the women continuously caressing the smooth oval shape of the brand they chose. When the same product was offered as a rectangular bar, it ranked much lower. Not once did consumers refer to the soap's shape or texture. They truly didn't know what was guiding their choice. Introspection may be a shaky base for our conclusions.

Friends (and enemies) who see us in action daily can often give us a more objective view of our motivations than we can ourselves. People who know of my passion for flying ascribe it to a hyperdeveloped quest for freedom. As one guy put it: "When you're up there in the sky, no one can get at you. You're free as a bird. That's real power." Hmm.

I suggest you pick two or three people who are close to you and explain the three motivations—nAch, nAff and nPow. Let your friends know you want an honest appraisal, and be careful not to put your thumb on the scale. I know one fellow who told his roommate that need for achievement is a compulsive grasp for money, need for power is a neurotic drive to put others in subjugation, and need for affiliation is warm affection reaching out in agape love. Then he asked, "Which do you see in me?" Guess what he heard!

If your own self-rating coincides with the judgment of others, you've probably spotted your preferred path to making life significant. There's a third method of discovering motivations you might find intriguing. It takes a bit of time, and it's not foolproof, but I think it's worth the effort. Look at the picture on page 66 for about twenty seconds. Then return here and continue reading.

Now take a paper and pencil and write an imaginative story about what you saw in the picture. Don't look at it again and don't write for longer than five minutes. You may find it helpful to consider these questions as guidelines:

☐ What is happening? Who are the people?

☐ What has led up to this situation? That is, what has happened in the past?

☐ What is being thought? What is wanted? By whom?

☐ What will happen? What will be done?

Stop reading now and take five minutes to do the exercise.[6]

The story you have made up can provide a clue to your motivational priority. It's fantasy, a kind of imagination that offers a window into your inner being. Of course this exercise gives no more than a glimpse. A more rigorous test would use multiple pictures and present them when you weren't thinking of motivation in general and nAch, nAff and nPow in particular.

People high in nAch tend to write stories about men and women wanting to do something better. For example, suppose the men in your story

© Punch—ROTHCO

"I'll race you!"

are magazine editors. If you said the man wearing glasses wants to edit articles faster, you may be high in nAch. Other typical nAch ingredients might have him wishing to outperform someone else (publish more gripping stories than the competition), achieve a personally set standard (finish by Friday), or do something unique (print an entire article that uses only the letters in the title of the publication; after all, this is fantasy). Or perhaps your need for achievement is reflected in your observation that he has worked hard at editing for a long time.

Lots of other things in your story could show you think in terms of achievement. Does a character blatantly state a need to accomplish a task? Does he do something to reach that goal? Are there personal or situational obstacles that hinder his success? Does he get help from anyone else in overcoming these problems? Does he anticipate success or failures if the goal isn't reached? Or, if the results are in, did you record his feelings of pleasure or discouragement? These concerns are additive. The more of them you built into the story, the more it reflects a high nAch.

Photo courtesy of David C. McClelland

"Wait a minute, Em," I can hear you say. "That's putting an awful big load on a simple story. What if I happened to write something completely different?"

In response I can only say, "You didn't."

Once I was discussing a vivid dream with a psychiatrist friend. I was rather embarrassed because it was filled with sex and violence. I tried to dismiss its significance with the disclaimer, "But after all, it's only a dream."

His response was kind but firm: "Yes—but it's *your* dream."

The story-writing exercise is called a Thematic Apperception Test—TAT for short.[7] The nAch-scoring criteria were validated on stories written by all kinds of people in achievement-oriented situations—students who had failed exams, businessmen receiving awards, athletes preparing to race. Over and over, the same features emerged. If your story was high in achievement imagery, it may mean only that you've been tossed into an unusual situation that focuses all your attention on task accomplishment. But more likely it shows a propensity to find significance in life through achieving meaningful goals.

If you have a high nAff, you've likely written a different kind of story. Your account will feature at least one character who wants to establish, restore or maintain a close, warm, friendly relationship with someone else. Perhaps the man speaking is worried about his father's continued rejection. Or maybe the other man is daydreaming about cuddling with his wife when the work is over. The affiliation imagery doesn't have to be deep or heart-gripping. A desire for friendly social activity is sufficient. You may have written that the woman is hoping they'll ask her to join them.

Again, the more nAff components in your narrative, the greater the likelihood that you are motivated by a need for people in your life. Perhaps the characters in your story openly stated their desire for a better relationship, took some action to insure affiliation, or expressed their pleasure over the bond that already existed between them. If the two men anticipate a successful relationship despite some situation holding them apart, it's added evidence that you are motivated by nAff. These features consistently pop up in stories written by folks in the midst of relationally loaded situations—both positive and negative. Couples in love, students receiving letters from home and those excluded from groups all write stories high in nAff details.

A test like this one may be the only way to uncover a high need for power, because people consistently tend to overlook or deny a power drive. Stories with strong actions, powerful emotional responses, or expressed concerns for reputation all reveal high nPow. For example, perhaps the listener's apparent boredom aggravates the speaker; or maybe one of the men is offering unsolicited advice on how to condense a manuscript. One man may try to persuade the other one to do something for him, or perhaps they both voice a fear about what the woman thinks of them. Any of these features shows nPow: making a character state a need for impact on others or do something to create it; mentioning the obstacles a character must overcome in attaining a power goal; describing the help a character receives from others in achieving his goal; describing his anticipation of success or failure if the results aren't in, and his positive or negative feelings if they are; describing an increase or decrease in a character's prestige. As with achievement and affiliation indicators, the more of these present, the greater the indication of high nPow. Power imagery is often expressed by people whose power is in question, such as political candidates waiting for election returns and people who are badgered by pushy salesmen.

So What?
We investigate our motives so we can better predict our responses and flag dangers. How would my motives relate to my interest in flying ultralights?

If I'm high in need for achievement, I'll tend to see mastery of the small plane as another step up the ladder of successful accomplishments. This means I could tire of the sport once the challenge wears off. Maybe I should rent a plane rather than sink a lot of money into something that can hoist me only one rung up the ladder.

Constructing my own machine from scratch would provide great achievement satisfaction. Given my mechanical ability, however, any airplane I'd build would fly like an iron glider. Those high in nAch take only moderate risks, so this avenue is closed to me. I could satisfy desires for achievement by entering spot-landing competitions or flour-bag bombing for accuracy contests. People high in nAch will always contrive ways to test their skill.

I'd have to be on guard, however, not to push my capabilities or those of my machine past their limits. The laws of nature always win those contests. Flying to new places, striving for smoother stick control, gradually being able to handle higher crosswinds on landing—these are all ways of scratching the achievement itch.

If I'm high in nAff, I'd be dumb to sink my money into a single-seat plane that requires waving good-by when I take off. Of course I could fly solo while holding joint ownership of the aircraft, or I could use the time aloft as a ticket for long hours of "hangar flying" afterward with fellow pilots. The Experimental Aircraft Association sponsors a week-long fly-in in Wisconsin every year. The annual attendance of ten thousand suggests that a lot of aviators are high in nAff, and the friendly camp-meeting atmosphere bears this out.

But there's a simpler way of meeting relationship needs: I could fly a two-seater. For a person who's high in nAff, half the fun of flying is sharing the thrill with a friend. Two-seat ultralights are just coming onto the market. If I know I'm a people person, I can stiffen my resolve to wait until they're perfected.

High nPow could push me in either a childish or adult direction. I could try to impress folks with my derring-do by endless accounts of great flying feats. I could don a leather jacket, silk scarf and goggles like Snoopy, or I could try to amaze the crowd below with low-level acrobatics and "buzz jobs." Unfortunately, such antics usually have their impact on the ground.

There's nothing illegitimate about the surge of adrenalin that comes from beating gravity. If a passenger's squeal of delight mirrors that thrill, so much the better. But those high in nPow need to make sure they don't glory in producing squeals of another kind. Empathy may not be their long suit.

There are more mature ways of channeling a high nPow. I could try to influence fellow pilots to take greater pains for safety. I could work to convince the public at large that the most dangerous part of the flight is the drive to the airport. Or I could gain the respect of my passengers by close attention to preflight inspection and smooth flying technique.

Which need turns me on? As a matter of fact, all of them: I test high on all three motives, nAch, nAff and nPow. Those who know me agree. This is neither good nor bad. It just *is*. I will probably always be this way. It's almost impossible to change basic motivation. But understanding what goads me gives me more options. Once I understand the direction and extent of my basic urges, I'm free to choose how I'll respond.

This is true within the church as well as within individuals. People high in nPow tend to see evangelism as the supreme Christian goal. The pastor who is aware that not all believers share his innate desire to be a fisher of men may avoid loading guilt on those who do not have the gift of evangelism.

Likewise, those with a high nAff have an easier time sharing their lives in *koinonia* fellowship. It comes naturally to them. They need to be sensitive to those who are constitutionally fearful of intimacy. Group confession is not for everybody.

Those high in nAch are liable to place service above evangelism or fellowship. But valuable as *diakonia* is, our Lord's words to Martha (Lk 10:38-42) show that there are times to value other responses. Somehow we've got to glory in our own motivation without thinking everyone else should find God's best the same way.

Our basic motivation in life is to find meaning by living for God. But we aren't all the same, and that meaning comes from different sources for different people. What satisfies me may not satisfy you.

If everyone were the same, I could understand others through introspection. I could safely assume that each desire, emotion and belief within me was merely a copy of what everyone else experienced. It wouldn't be necessary to "walk a mile in another man's moccasins," as the Indian proverb suggests. The only reason for me to write the next four chapters would be to bring this book to a respectable length.

But understanding thee is a separate skill from understanding me. To communicate effectively I need to be able to spot and appreciate our differences. The next section of the book seeks to provide tools for that task.

I'm glad we're not clones with lock-step desires. How boring that would be. But it's important to know *how* we're different. Then we can leave the multitudes of the unconscious driven and join the ranks of those who are knowingly drawn.

UNDERSTANDING
THEE

4
PERCEPTION

*People communicate
to reduce uncertainty.*

W E DON'T KNOW WHO discovered water, but we're pretty sure it wasn't the fish."[1] I like this bit of wry wisdom. It points out that, immersed in our own reality, we often fail to notice its impact on us. We're likely to ignore air until a stuffy nose, acrid smell or high wind literally brings us to our senses. Likewise, we are unaware of the "perceptual glasses" through which we look out at the world. Because these glasses color everything we see, what we see is not necessarily what we get. Yet we're usually blissfully ignorant of the biases that affect our impressions of other people.

Have you heard the story of the three umpires talking shop? The first ump says, "Some's balls and some's strikes—I calls 'em as they is." The second ump knows the game isn't quite that simple. "Some's balls and some's strikes," he says; "I calls 'em as I sees 'em." The third ump understands that reality is in the eye of the beholder. He says, "Some's balls and some's strikes—but they ain't nothin' till I calls 'em."[2]

This chapter is about how we "calls 'em." Perception isn't just a simple matter of observing other people. It's a process of drawing inferences, making judgments, reaching conclusions; a process that not only labels people but also changes them. This past year I spent a month in the Philippine Islands. It was an intensive time of meeting people, at least five hundred new faces and names. As a fish out of water—a foreigner trying to relate in a new culture—I was more aware of the quirks of human perception than I normally am. I'll use some of my experiences to illustrate established principles of impression formation. But one caution first.

A Bible translator went to a remote tribe to provide the Scripture in their own tongue. He spent nearly a year with the one bilingual informant he could find in order to learn the grammar and vocabulary of the language. He noted many structural repetitions—the same sound recurring three or four times in sequence. Then his work all caved in—he discovered his informant stuttered.

To the best of my ability the rest of this chapter presents a reliable perceptual guide. But beware. I may stutter. There's no sure-fire, money-back, guaranteed authentic map of reality out there. When it comes to people perception, we're all ultimately on our own.

The Myth of Sameness

You'd think it would have been easy for me to anticipate differences between myself and the Filipinos I met. The mere fact that I flew through ten time zones to a tropical climate should have given me a clue. I knew we'd have differences in physical stature and skin color. But I guess down deep I expected the folks to be just like me. Perhaps I was fooled by the apparent ease of communication. English is the official language of the Islands, and American rock music seems to have the same status. Or maybe I assumed that shared love for Jesus Christ would blot out dissimilarities. Whatever the reason, I made a common human error—I subconsciously assumed others would react like me. Wrong!

Figure 1 shows a classic outline of the different values that are held by different cultures. Clyde Kluckholn looked at three positions in five areas: view of human nature, relationship of man to God or nature, sense of time, type of activity, and structure of social relationships.[3]

Figure 1. Kluckholn's Table of Values

Orientation ◄─────────────── Range ───────────────►

Orientation			
View of Human Nature	Evil	Mixed	Good
Relationship of man to God/Nature	Nature over man	Cooperative	Man subdues nature
Sense of time	Past	Present	Future
Type of activity	Being	Growing	Doing
Structure of social relationships	Authoritarian	Group	Individualistic

In three of these five crucial values, my hosts saw the world differently from this middle-American, McDonaldized guy.

My sense of time was different from theirs. I'm very future oriented—constantly making plans, scheduling, blocking things out on my calendar. Seeing time as a commodity that might slip away, I begin to feel anxious when next week's activities aren't firm. The Filipinos I met were more apt to focus on the present. They would not think about a future activity until the present event was completed.

Activity itself had a different importance. I was raised to value action, accomplishment, achievement. When I was at an InterVarsity camp in college I heard a speaker say, "God is more interested in what you are than in what you do." Every nerve fiber within me cried out no. The speaker wouldn't have drawn that reaction in the Philippines.

But it was in the relational area that Filipino values stood out against mine in bold relief. I found a strong group orientation that was quite different from typical Western individualism. If one person was late for a meeting, the others would usually wait before beginning. They didn't want anyone to feel left out. As in America, a speaker would work to establish eye contact with each person present. But listeners would do the same

Drawing by M. Twohy. © 1983 The New Yorker Magazine, Inc.

thing, constantly scanning the group so everyone would be included. To gaze solely at the speaker would be considered rude. A group of three or four people might take up to an hour to disengage itself from a larger body. Good-byes were filled with warm touch and laughter. If one person wasn't quite ready to go, the other two or three would wait unhurriedly. Often they'd get drawn back in. I love this concern for others that Filipinos constantly show.

Another aspect of the high value placed on group allegiance caused me to swallow hard. I spoke at the commissioning service of interns at a Bible college. After the address each student came forward and knelt before the college president and the district superintendent. These men placed their hands on the students' heads and solemnly announced where they would be spending the next year in pioneer ministry. ("The Lord has called you to go the Sarangani!") The students had no vote and no advance notice concerning where they were sent. As corporate guidance goes, this is major-league hard ball. All the students answered that they would obey God's will, and three days later they left on their assignments. I believe their response not only was an act of faithful obedience, but also reflected their cultural value of group solidarity. One reason this ceremony had a profound impact on me was my subconscious expectation that these students would be just like me. In this case I couldn't help spotting the differences between us. Often, however, we never notice them.

The Power of Expectation

Take a look at the picture on page 80.[4] What do you see? The face of an old woman with a pointed chin, or a stylishly dressed young lady in profile? The drawing can be viewed either way. I've shown it to lots of people, and two-thirds see the hag while one-third see the fashion model. Take another look and try to catch the alternative figure. If you're having trouble, blink your eyes a few times. If you still see only the old crone, concentrate on her nose. This line traces the entire face of the young lady. Translate the other way if you see only the finely clothed lady. Her face defines the nose of the old woman.

This picture is intentionally ambiguous. I ran an informal experiment with it in class this year. I split the students into two discussion groups. One group considered the medical plight of the elderly; the other discussed new trends in fashion design. About fifteen minutes into the discussion I showed them the picture, and they recorded their impressions. Everyone in the group considering Medicare saw an old woman, while most of those in the fashion discussion recognized a young lady. The topics created a frame of reference which shaped their perceptions. Subconsciously they figured it would be natural for me to show them a picture connected with the discussion. They saw what they expected to see.

A similar thing happened to my wife the fateful day I shaved off my beard. Although I was cleanshaven when we married, for fifteen years

Jeanie had lived with a face accented by hair. One day when I was out of town I shaved it off. Disappointed that Jeanie wasn't home when I got back in town, I grabbed a rake and started pulling leaves from the bushes—an activity I perform at least once or twice a decade. A half-hour later Jeanie pulled into the driveway, got out of the car and nodded absently as she walked by me no more than six feet away. I crashed into her world when I called out, "Honey . . ." She stared at me as if I were from outer space.

Jeanie later claimed that ten per cent of the problem was that she didn't have her contacts in, thirty per cent was due to my altered appearance, and a whopping sixty per cent of her failure to recognize me was that I was working around the house. Em is not the kind of guy to be puttering in the garden—so this man must be someone else. We see what we expect to see.

Perceptual bias worked to my advantage when I went to meet with leaders in the tribal Bible school. The school was hard to reach, and it was nestled in a community where antigovernment communist activity was high. For this reason, few Christians— nationals or otherwise—would make the effort to get there. Since I was only the second Caucasian to visit in the last fifteen years, the writer of two books that they'd read and an American Ph.D., the faculty and students expected me to be the greatest thing since the apostle Paul. Needless to say, I wasn't. I spoke much too briefly the first time I addressed them: they wanted at least an hour. I refused food the first time it was offered—a really gauche move, I later learned. But no difference. Their expectations were so high that I honestly couldn't fail. We see what we expect to see.

Sometimes those expectations are shaped by what we want. In a classic study in social perception, people were shown a picture of an incident on a New York subway for a few seconds.[5] Two men stood in the foreground. One was white, one black. One wore a business suit, the other laborer's clothes. One held an open razor in a threatening manner, the other appeared scared. Many white subjects who viewed the picture reported that a black laborer was robbing a white executive. Actually it was the black man dressed in the business suit and the white man holding the razor. But this not only violated the viewers' expectations, it ran counter to what they thought *ought* to be happening. Motives affect perception.

Selective perception comes into play any time we have a stake in the outcome. Two grown men can observe the same sports event and see different games. The other day I was standing beside another man at a tennis match. We consistently disagreed. When I thought a ball was on

"I'm happy to say that my final judgment of a case is almost always consistent with my prejudgment of the case."

the line, he thought it was wide. When I saw it out, he saw it in. As it turned out neither of us was a disinterested party. Our daughters were playing against each other.

Not only do we see what we want to see; we also often see what we fear. When Sharon was three years old she once woke up in the middle of the night with a bloodcurdling scream. I dashed into her room expecting to see at the very least an ogre hiding in the closet. As a matter of fact that's what Sharon expected too. She pointed fearfully at a form swaying in the door. It did look a bit like a monster—but when I turned on the light we saw it was only a coat on a hanger being blown by a summer breeze. It reminds me of the old verse:

> As I was going up the stair
> I met a man who wasn't there
> He wasn't there again today
> I wish, I wish he'd go away.[6]

Only One Shot at First Impressions

First impressions stick. We tend to give much more weight to the first things we learn about other people than we do to later information.[7] This is called the *law of primacy*. How does it work? Let's suppose your first impression of me is that I'm warm. That's nice. Later on you're exposed to some negative information indicating that I'm lazy. The law of primacy suggests you'll think of the warm Em Griffin as the real me and discount the laziness as a one-time problem due to peculiar circumstances. If my laziness affects your judgment of me at all, you'll probably assimilate it into your overall positive view. In this case: Warm + Lazy = Relaxed.

If, however, you start out with the belief that I'm lazy, this judgment will color all the other input you get about me. Any personal warmth I show will be interpreted in light of my sloth. For example, it may seem like a ploy to cover up my lack of industry. In that case: Lazy + Warm = Conniving.

First impressions are hard to shake. I find this true when I'm on a faculty selection committee. If the first thing I hear about a candidate has a negative tone, I discount all the superlative praise in subsequent conversations. If the first reference is unabashedly positive, however, I'm willing to dismiss later negative data as mere evidence of the candidate's humanness. We expect the second and third impressions to be consistent with the first, and we're quite capable of filtering our perceptions to guarantee that they are. I think I did this with Lena in the Philippines.

Lena struck me as a delightfully warm young woman with a mature and vibrant faith. How did I reach that conclusion? My first encounter with her was at an informal time of group prayer on a Manila beach. She urged us to join hands and said, "Let us remember as we pray that Jesus is here with us." Later as we were walking by a Roman Catholic chapel she excused herself for a moment and dashed in to light a candle for her boyfriend.

Now this plain vanilla Midwestern evangelical had always lumped candle-lighting with indulgences for sin and plastic dashboard statues of Jesus. Yet in this case I saw it merely as an extension of genuine devotion rather than a cultic practice. Why did the first impression overrule the second?

We have a tremendous need to hold a consistent world view. Contradictory evidence, loose ends and unresolved differences are threats to our sense of order. So it's quite possible we'll scrutinize early cues about another in forming an impression, but tend to ignore later material that might call our initial judgment into question. The official term to designate this process is *attention decrement.*[8]

Or perhaps we pay just as much attention to later input as to the first pieces of evidence, but assign it to different causes. In this way I could attribute Lena's prayer life to her inner conviction and discount her candle-lighting as the result of her cultural upbringing over which she had no control. Whatever the reason, the final impression I formed of this young Christian wasn't a sum of equally weighted bits of information. Consider how my judgment might have been altered if the first encounter had been by the chapel rather than on the beach. As a missionary friend who is quite sensitive to cross-cultural issues puts it, "You only get to make a first impression once."

Distracted by the Down Side

Gossip makes hypocrites of us all. We condemn it publicly yet strain to hear the latest dirt, and our aural antenna twitch all the more when the news of another is bad. The negative has a greater impact than the positive.

It's hard to say why this is so. Maybe we're more certain of the things we hate than of the things we want to embrace. ("I don't know what I want to do with my life, but I sure don't want to . . .") Possibly we hear so many good things that the occasional critical comment sticks out. Or perhaps it's just sheer cussedness—human sinfulness. Whatever it is, we tend to give greater weight to a single negative impression than to a cluster of positive ones.

While in the Philippines I spent three days inspecting a dozen development projects fostered by the Institute for International Development,

Inc. (IIDI), a Christian organization which tries to combat hunger in Third World countries by making loans of a few thousand dollars to small entrepreneurs so they can expand their businesses. IIDI has found that an infusion of a thousand dollars' capital can create a new job that can feed a family of six indefinitely. Nice bang for the buck. On one of my visits I met a man who was the model of Christian grace. His manufacturing plant was clean, his product was high quality, and he was reported to be a pillar of his church community. But I couldn't shake off an inner distaste once I found out he hadn't hired additional workers since receiving his loan. One negative blotted out all the positives.

The same thing happens with letters of recommendations—those blatant attempts to create a positive impression. When I read such a letter I gloss over the praise and zero in on the doubtful comments. This kind of screening, however, can lead to selecting less qualified job seekers. I once sat on a church committee selecting candidates for a summer missions project. Thirty-five college kids applied for fifteen positions. Each applicant brought letters of recommendation and took part in a twenty-minute face-to-face interview with the committee. After the whole process we met in an all-day session to decide who should go abroad. Some of the candidates had great strengths. But those with particular aptitudes or strong personality traits usually evidenced a weakness or two as well. We passed over this type of person every time in favor of the fellow or girl who was less qualified but had no observable faults. We had meant to pick the best, but because of the human tendency to pay too much attention to the negative, we ended up selecting the least objectionable.

In many cultures, the crucial issue in people perception is cold vs. warm. An individual can have stellar characteristics, but an impression of coolness will disqualify him or her for further intimacy. One survival manual in cross-cultural living lists "a sense of humor" as the key ingredient in avoiding culture shock.[9] Laughter and warmth are kissing cousins.

An early incident with the Belah-an Bible School leaders set the tone for our later interpersonal relations. A former student of mine was telling me that I didn't need to worry about health matters while we were on this tribe's remote islands. "They use herbal medicines," she said with a solemn

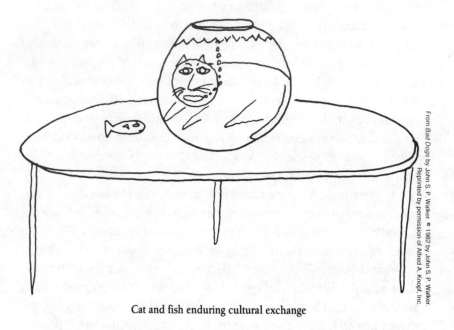

From *Bad Dogs* by John S. P. Walker. © 1982 by John S. P. Walker. Reprinted by permission of Alfred A. Knopf, Inc.

Cat and fish enduring cultural exchange

nod. She then proceeded to relate how a shoulder pain was cured overnight with the use of kerosene. Now that brought a smile to my face. Somehow I've never classified kerosene as an herb. Having worked with diesel engines, I also know the pungent odor of fuel oil. After a few seconds I couldn't hold back. "Aw, Maria," I said, "it wasn't the medicinal property of the kerosene that made the difference. It was the stink. Here's what happened. After you rubbed it in you smelled so bad that Juan [her husband] let you alone for a while, and your shoulder healed itself."

That brand of earthy corn may not do anything for you, but my native hosts roared with laughter. They told me later that it was at that point they decided it would be okay to laugh together and touch each other—something we did almost constantly during the next days. For good interpersonal relations with members of that group, perception of warmth is crucial.

Find the Feeling
But how skilled are we at picking up on what's going on inside another

person? If another's thoughts are the issue, the answer is, "Not very." A few years back I was one of eight participants in an intensive seminar on social perception. We spent over thirty-six hours sharing our histories, life situations, dreams and feelings toward everything imaginable. At lunch the last day we tried an experiment to see how well we knew what the other folks were thinking. We all wrote down the three thoughts uppermost in our minds, then folded the paper and passed it around to the right. Before reading it, the person receiving the list wrote down three guesses as to what his partner had in mind.

We wanted to do well. No one tried to fake out the others. Yet when the thoughts and the predictions were placed side by side, even a charitable interpretation could find overlap in only three cases. Three out of twenty four—we aren't very good at mind reading!

Picking up on another's mood, however, is well within our reach. Facial expression, body posture and tone of voice can clearly display the affect a person is feeling. I run a classroom demonstration on communication of emotional meaning in which I select three students to act out different emotions— anger, joy, surprise, fear, admiration and so on—while counting from 1 to 10. This is my attempt to give them something to say that is content neutral. There's nothing inherently pleasurable or disgusting in reciting numbers; the feeling has to come from the nonverbal signals the actor puts out. The audience uses a checklist of twelve emotions to use to describe the feeling that comes across. Here are the consistent results:

1. People can accurately identify emotional mood states without words at a rate much higher than chance would explain. In fact about seventy-five per cent of the time they nail the mood state intended by the actors. Of course the actors are trying to portray certain feelings. That percentage may well be lower when people aren't making an effort to communicate their feelings—and it certainly is lower when they make a conscious attempt to hide them.

2. Some people are vastly superior to others in identifying emotions. Females generally do much better than males in this type of exercise. In one of my classes the girl with the worst score still did better than the guy with the highest. Perhaps in a society that is just beginning to share power equally,

"No, Charles, I don't have a cold. What you hear in my voice is contempt."

a woman's ability to accurately interpret another's mood is a strong survival skill. Fortunately, it seems to be a skill that can be improved over time.

3. Some emotions are much easier to pick up on than others. Figure 2 divides the twelve moods I used into four categories: pleasurable or distressing, active or passive. By far the easiest to spot are in the active/distressing box (fear, anger, disgust). Observers almost always identify them correctly. On the other hand, the passive/pleasurable feelings of love, admiration and satisfaction are often missed. Half the time they are merely confused with each other, but half the time they are labeled boredom or dislike. The implications are obvious: if two people like each other but

Figure 2. Perception of Emotions

	Pleasurable	Distressing
Active	Surprise	Fear
	Happiness	Anger
	Laughter	Disgust
Passive	Love	Dislike
	Admiration	Sadness
	Satisfaction	Boredom

never give voice to their affection, there's a good chance at least one of them will miss it. Yet if one party is temporarily upset by the other, it will come through loud and clear, even without a word spoken. Remedy: If you feel positive toward someone—say it!

Holding Others Responsible

While in the Philippines I stayed overnight in a poor rural village. My hosts asked me to join them at a meeting of their agricultural co-op. This was a voluntary association of farmers to provide revolving credit for seed and bulk buying power. These hard-working people were justifiably proud of their effort. They invited me to ask questions about their experience. "What was the biggest mistake you made in your first year?" I asked.

Dumb! I had only just met them. I was a foreign visitor before whom they wanted to look good. I hadn't earned the right to raise such a sensitive issue. Every head bowed, every eye turned away. When I finally realized my mistake I wondered what my hosts would think of me. Would they think I meant to embarrass them, or would they chalk it off as a well-intentioned American who didn't know any better? As it turned out they gave me the benefit of the doubt—a visitor's pass, as it were. But judging intentions, just like perceiving actions, is open to bias.

We tend to assume that others have more freedom of action than they really do.[10] Thus when the disciples see the blind man they automatically ask: "Who sinned, this man or his parents?" (Jn 9:2). Note that outside

"The jury has found you guilty, but, if it's any consolation, you sure had me fooled."

forces or pure chance are discounted as possible explanations. They hold the firm conviction that someone is directly accountable. We're no different. We want to assign praise or blame.

I saw this happen every time my son played hockey. Jim was the goalie and needed little reminder from the coach when things went poorly. Every mistake he made showed up on the scoreboard. Every time the puck went into the net there were three possibilities: the shot was too tough, Jim didn't have the skill to stop it or Jim wasn't trying. On the face of it, the third explanation seems the most far-fetched. Jim loves hockey, wants to win and has a strong desire to look good in front of the crowd. The explanation that he was playing against some talented guys or that he doesn't have the quickest reactions in the world appears much more plausible. But every time a goal was scored the coach would bellow, "Come on, Jimmy, you've got to try harder!"

Of course this can break the other way too. One time Jim made a sideways lunge, tripped over his stick and tossed his arm out for balance. By sheer blind luck the puck struck and lodged in his outstretched glove. The fans went wild and the coach shouted his pleasure at the super save. "Now you're really putting out, Jimmy." In both cases the coach overemphasized Jim's responsibility.

Coaches aren't the only ones to assume a player meant to do everything that happens. In his sensitive novel _The Chosen,_ Chaim Potok recounts a baseball game between two Jewish teams. Reuven is pitching when Danny hits a line drive. The ball smashes into Reuven's glasses and puts him in the hospital. Even though sick, Reuven's father visits his injured son.

"You're not taking care of yourself, abba."

"I am worried about my baseball player." He smiled at me. "I worry all the time you will get hit by a taxi or a trolley car and you go and get hit by a baseball."

"I hate that Danny Saunders for this. He's making you sick."

"Danny Saunders is making me sick? How is he making me sick?"

"He deliberately aimed at me, abba. He hit me deliberately. Now you're getting sick worrying about me."

My father looked at me in amazement. "He hit you deliberately?"

"You should see how he hits. He almost killed Schwartzie. He said his team would kill us apikorsim."

"Apikorsim?"

"They turned the game into a war."

"I do not understand. On the telephone Reb Saunders said his son was sorry."

"Sorry! I'll bet he's sorry! He's sorry he didn't kill me altogether!"

My father gazed at me intently, his eyes narrowing. I saw the look of amazement slowly leave his face.

"I do not like you to talk that way," he said sternly.

"It's true, abba."

"Did you ask him if it was deliberate?"

"No."

"How can you say something like that if you are not sure? That is a terrible thing to say." He was controlling his anger with difficulty.

"It seemed to be deliberate."

"Things are always what they seem to be, Reuven? Since when?"[11]

Our natural tendency to read purpose into others' actions is especially strong in some situations. One such case is when the results are bad—as they were for Reuven. We look at the down-and-out bum and label him lazy. We see the successful business tycoon and call him lucky. Note that we attribute greater moral responsibility to the person who does poorly than to the one who does well.[12]

Another way we read purpose into people's actions is to assume they will act only out of self-interest. I led the Young Life club in my community for ten years. The first three years I was on the paid staff of this Christian organization. The final seven I led the club as a nonpaid volunteer. My work seemed to have greater impact on the kids when it wasn't my official job. Somehow I came across as more sincere when I had no apparent motive for my witness. When there's no visible payoff for our action, others are confident we chose freely.

We tend to see others as free agents who voluntarily choose to do exactly what they do. We adopt the world view reflected in this ditty from *Alice in Wonderland*:

Speak roughly to your little boy,
And beat him when he sneezes.
He only does it to annoy,
Because he knows it teases.[13]

To counteract this natural leaning we would do well to be cautious about jumping to conclusions about other people's intentions. As my favorite seminary professor, Ed Carnell, was fond of saying: "People are victims as well as subjects."

The sneeze may not have been voluntary. A virus, high pollen count or whiff of pepper, not the desire to irritate, may have been its cause. It's a healthy sign of Christian maturity when we entertain some degree of doubt as to another's motivation.

Giving Ourselves a Pass

We have no problem being charitable to ourselves. Although we overemphasize others' moral responsibility, we have a much more lenient yardstick to use on ourselves. We tend to give ourselves the benefit of the doubt and blame outside forces, other people or sunspots for our own behavior. The excuses we give reflect this bias. I've heard each of the following statements in the last two weeks, some from my own lips. All of them tacitly say, "Don't blame me, I didn't have any choice in the matter." The statements in parentheses are what could have been said if the speaker had wanted to present a realistic picture.

"That's just the way I am." (I choose to be this way.)

"I can't help it." (I don't want to change.)

"Due to circumstances beyond our control . . " (We goofed.)

"It's not fair." (I don't like it.)

"You make me mad." (I make myself mad.)

"The test was impossible." (I didn't study very hard.)

"I need to . . ." (I want to . . .)

This bias toward ourselves is built right into the structure of some languages. Suppose I dropped a glass of water on the floor and wanted to report the fact in Spanish. I'd say, "Se me cayo el vaso," which literally means "The glass dropped itself." This semantic dodge nicely avoids any ownership of my part in the puddle.

We don't duck responsibility all the time. Most folks are willing to be held accountable when things turn out well. There's lots of "I" talk when the results are good:[14]

"I won the game with a home run."

"I was the life of the party."

"I led him to the Lord."

But we seldom admit our contribution when someone forsakes the faith. "I led him astray" would be a hard truth to grasp privately, much less put into words.

Since our natural tendency is to underestimate our freedom, it's helpful to try to err on the side of choice. I've already spoken of Viktor Frankl, a psychiatrist who survived the Auschwitz death camp. He's my model of personal accountability. If anyone ever had the right to plead lack of freedom, it would be this victim of Nazi oppression. But to Frankl this would be a cop-out. "Each man is questioned by life; and he can only answer to life by answering for his own life; to life he can only respond by being responsible. [I see] in responsibleness the very essence of human existence![15]

Let's sum up. The big issue in person perception is not optics. Most of us have physiological equipment that far surpasses the capabilities of a video recorder. But values, motives, past experiences, hopes and prejudices all distort images of others before they even register on our brain pan. We all have our personal perceptual quirks, and we all seem to share the following systematic biases:

1. We assume others will react to the world just as we do.

2. What we expect to see strongly colors what we do see.

3. We give undue weight to first impressions.

4. Negative data make a bigger impact on us than positive information.

5. It's easier to spot others' displeasure than their satisfaction.

6. We attribute more freedom of action to others than they really have.

7. We hold ourselves less responsible for our actions than the situation warrants.

Awareness of these tendencies is half the battle against getting sucked in by them. Once we realize the typical twists we give our perceptions, we can no longer naively assume that the person we see is the one who's there. That's good. It gets even better when we develop a plan of attack to gain an impression that's closer to reality.

"Our biggest problem around here is lack of information. Of course,
I have nothing to base that on."

It's not without reason that I've illustrated most of the material in this chapter from my Philippine experience. I like to treat every new interpersonal encounter as a cross-cultural experience. That's hard when there are no plane tickets, passports or physical dissimilarities. But if I think of myself as a stranger in a strange land who has to sniff out the culture, I seem to get a more reliable picture of the other person. Since most of us haven't worked as cultural anthropologists, let me switch the metaphor.

We get the best information about others when we play detective. Good detectives try not to jump to conclusions. They realize that situations and people are often more complicated than they appear at first glance, and so they seek more clues. They wait till all the evidence is in before they reach a judgment. Competent investigators avoid the temptation to mind read. They ask lots of questions about people, listen to the answers and ask some more. All the time they are listening and watching to pick up new data. The following chapters on listening to language and picking up nonverbal cues will help you develop your sensitivities in these areas.

I hope that all this sounds suspiciously Christian. In his famous chapter on love Paul captures the truth about person perception: "Now we see through a glass darkly" (1 Cor 13:12 KJV). Until such time as we see clearly face to face, the remedy to murky images is to be patient and kind, bearing all things, believing all things, hoping all things. In God's economy, accuracy is enhanced by love.

Yet even loving eyes will miss the fullness of another's humanness. I've been guilty of this with Jean. I'm finishing this chapter on the twenty-fifth anniversary of our wedding. We've often sought counseling help to improve the quality of our marriage. Recently I made the statement, "Jeanie isn't much on fuss when it comes to celebrating anniversaries." Our counseling friend said, "Could you restate that, Em? Put it this way: *My* Jeanie isn't much on fuss when it comes to celebrating anniversaries." It sounded awkward and possessive. But I tried it on for size. I suddenly realized that what I was treating as absolute truth might be a faulty perception. I checked it out with the source and discovered Jeanie wanted a lot of hoopla. "I'd like some fuss," she said when asked. So tonight we're going out to dinner and a play. The evening includes a present and some flowers.

I think I'm seeing things a bit more clearly.

5

LISTENING TO LANGUAGE

*Words don't mean things;
people mean things.*

IN HIS MARVELOUS BOOK *The Friendship Factor* Alan Loy McGinnis has a chapter called "How to Improve Your Conversational Skill." I think most folks read that heading and assume the chapter gives tips on how to tell a story, increase vocabulary or come up with a witty response. But it doesn't. The chapter is about listening.

Listening is a low-status occupation. As one who does a lot of public speaking, I'm well aware that society places a high cash value on the ability to present an idea in a clear and interesting way. Except for psychiatrists, most listeners don't get that kind of payoff. It's the same with the written word. Nine months ago I committed myself to two tasks—finishing this book and reading fifty classic novels. As I get close to reaching both goals my colleagues appear more impressed with the first. Sending seems more important than receiving. But is it?

McGinnis recounts the story of a woman who had successive meals with two of England's great leaders. She said that when she left the dining room

after sitting next to Mr. Gladstone, she thought he was the cleverest person in England. But after sitting next to Mr. Disraeli, she felt like *she* was.[1] One can imagine which man talked and which listened.

Jeanie accuses me of tricking her during our first few dates. She had discovered an infallible way of getting a guy to enjoy their time together and ask her out again. She'd ask questions about his life and then soak up the answers. Apparently I was the first one who turned the tables on her by wanting to hear her story.

"To be a man, a man must have his say." But it doesn't do any good if no one is willing to listen. A family sat down in a restaurant and contemplated the menu. After taking the grown-ups' order the waitress turned to the seven-year-old boy and asked what he'd like. Up to this point in his life no one had ever cared to know, so he hesitated. And before he uttered a sound his mother answered, "Junior will have creamed chipped beef on whole wheat toast." The waitress's eyes never left the boy.

"Would you like a hamburger?" ("Yes.")

"Want cheese on it?" ("No.")

"Catsup and relish?" ("Yes.")

As the waitress headed toward the kitchen the kid turned to his folks and exclaimed, "Gee, she thinks I'm alive."

Real listening is a high-participation endeavor. Perhaps that's why the Chinese ideograph for the verb *to listen* is made up of symbols for the words *ears, eyes, you, individual attention* and *heart*.[2] The men in my family have always had high blood pressure. Every once in a while I'll take out a sphygmographic cuff to spot-monitor mine. I find it's often up ten points if I take it after really tracking with a student who has poured out his concerns. If on the other hand I've switched into neutral and practiced what Jesus called "listening without hearing," the needle stays pegged at the base rate. (Caution: the Surgeon General has determined that listening can be hazardous to your health.)

Empathic listening takes more than sheer effort, however. It requires a certain mindset or attitude to successfully take the role of the other person. I'd encourage you to invest ten minutes responding to the exercise in the box below. It could give you an estimate of your native ability to hear what another is saying.

Personal Description Survey

Think of two different people who are roughly your own age—one whom you like, the other whom you dislike. It's important that you think of two specific individuals by name. Spend a few moments looking over the two names, mentally comparing and contrasting the people you have in mind. Think of their habits, their beliefs, their mannerisms, their relations to others and the characteristics they have which you most often use to describe them to other people.

Write the name of the person you like at the top of a blank sheet of paper. Now describe this person as fully as you can. Put down any and all characteristics which would help another understand who this person really is. Please spend only about five minutes listing these attributes.

Now go ahead and do the same thing for the person you don't like. List all of the habits, beliefs, ways of treating others, mannerisms and personal characteristics you can think of. Again, limit yourself to five minutes.

You're probably wondering what this has to do with listening. The exercise is aimed at assessing cognitive complexity. Some people see the world in black and white. There are good guys and bad guys. This two-valued way of thinking is captured by a wry observation: "There are two kinds of people in the world—those who think there are two kinds of people in the world . . . and those who don't." Others can see shades of gray. They see people as mixtures and blends of many categories. This is where sensitive listening comes in. The more shades of meaning a person can handle, the more she is able to listen to another's account without jumping to conclusions.

The survey is easy to score.[3] For each person you described, merely count the number of separate concepts you listed. For purposes of measuring cognitive complexity, it makes no difference what you said about the other person, only how many different ideas you presented. If you described the person as shy, that's one. If you went on to say he doesn't talk much, that's two. Using both terms shows that you see a shade of difference between shyness and silence. Score a point for each separate term you used to describe the person you like. Ditto with the person you don't like. When in doubt, give yourself a point. The only terms you don't credit are neutral physical descriptions that say nothing about the other's personality or social role. That is, items such as tall, brown hair, twenty-eight years old, policeman or president of the Lions Club don't get a point. Finally, add the two scores for a total index of cognitive complexity.

A range of 20-25 is about average. If you scored above that it's probably a good indication that you can handle many shades of interpersonal meaning. This won't automatically make you a good listener. That requires conscious effort as well. But it does suggest that your mindset doesn't pigeonhole everything you hear into only a few mental slots. If you put down fewer than twenty terms, it may mean you have a tendency to lump together a whole lot of different responses. Being aware of that can be your ticket to change. It's possible to cultivate the knack of seeing life's gradations and complexities. That's what a liberal arts education is all about—understanding what it's like to be another person, in another time, in another place.

Some Christians are suspicious of the ability to see multiple facets of the same person. They argue that Christ himself saw the world in either/or terms. Didn't he say, "He who is not with me is against me, and he who does not gather with me scatters" (Mt 12:30)? Yes. But at another time he cautioned, "Whoever is not against us is for us" (Mk 9:40). And he reserved his strongest criticism for those who divided the world into sinners and saints—the Pharisees.

Some of Jesus' stories suggest that we'll have to wait until the end times to sort out the genuineness of people's response toward him (see, for example, the parable of the wheat and the tares in Matthew 13:24-30 and the account of the last judgment in Matthew 25:31-46). Even if we're basic red-yellow-blue people who have a tough time seeing the subtle hues of the spectrum, we can be better listeners if we hold off judgment till a later date. Otherwise we're in danger of being about as helpful as Job's comforters.

"OK," you say, "I realize how much my relationship with other people depends on picking up what they're trying to communicate. I want to hear them out without jumping to preset conclusions. I understand that this kind of listening takes as much effort as speaking, and in my better moments, I'm willing to invest the energy. But language is slippery. I'll hear words that strike me one way and later find out my friend meant something completely different. Help me get a handle on how to interpret what I hear. Give me some hints on how to discover what people's words really mean."

I'll try.

Words: What Do They Mean?

Let's start with a story. When my son was one year old we went to the park. Jim's face lit up in delight when he saw a squirrel. With unsteady toddler steps he set out to reach the furry animal. I'm not sure whether he wanted to pat it, squeeze it or taste it. But his outstretched arms left no question he wanted to touch it. The squirrel seemed unconcerned until the midget man got within six feet. Then he scampered off to a safe distance. My son changed direction and doggedly plodded toward the squirrel's new position. This happened repeatedly for about twenty minutes until the squirrel got tired of the game and jumped about four feet up the trunk of a big tree.

Not knowing he'd lost, Jim moved toward the tree. When he got too close for comfort the squirrel scurried to the other side. The oak now hid the critter from Jim's view, but Em Griffin didn't father any dumb kids. Jim knew the squirrel was on the other side, so he staggered around the tree to bring him back in sight. The wily squirrel, however, was more clever than the one-year-old. As Jim made his unsteady path to the right around the tree, the squirrel matched his pace along the back, always keeping the tree between himself and the persistent kid. The net effect was that Jim walked around the tree three times without ever catching a glimpse of the animal. Finally his legs wouldn't take him any farther. He sat down, gazing at the tree, looking totally bewildered.

Figure 3. A Squirrelly Problem

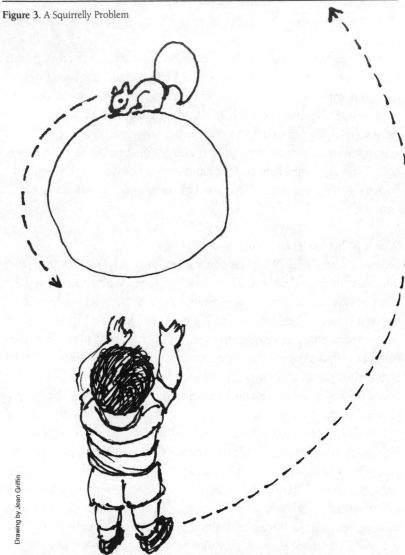

Drawing by Jean Griffin

I've tried to paint a word picture for you as illustrated in figure 3. I hope we share the same visual image of "The Great Squirrel Mystery." Now let me ask you a question that can be just as baffling to us as the squirrel's disappearance was to Jim:

During all his torturous walking, did Jim go around the squirrel?

"Who cares?" you say. Granted, the issue doesn't rank with matters such as nuclear proliferation or how to reduce the national deficit, but it's a problem that people from William James to the present have discussed.[4] I've had students argue heatedly on both sides of the question. What do you think? Yes or no, did Jim go around the squirrel?

I could make a case for either side. Even though they couldn't see each other, Jim and the squirrel were always facing each other. Add the fact that the squirrel was also moving, and it's obvious that Jim did not go around the squirrel. On the other hand, Jim etched a circular path that enclosed the animal. It's obvious that Jim did go around the squirrel.

So what is the problem? It isn't lack of evidence. Everyone agrees on the facts. The problem is ambiguity. What does "go around" mean? If it refers to sequentially moving to the north—east—south—west of an object, then my boy went around the squirrel. If it means facing the belly—right side—back—left side of the animal, then he never went around the squirrel.

The Jim/squirrel go-around isn't an isolated case of ambiguity. We face it in some of our most cherished words. Take justice, for example. Almost all people are for it, but what are they for? To some *justice* means people getting what they deserve. To others it means everyone getting the same. A third group sees justice as each person getting what he needs. Imagine the confusion when meritorians, egalitarians and necessitarians sling the term at each other.

The word *love* is no better. It's been so oozed, used and abused that it may not have any specific referent. Love becomes a feeling you feel you're feeling when you feel you're feeling a feeling. Scripture often steps down from that lofty level of abstraction and explains global concepts in terms of concrete behavior.

Love: "Greater love has no one than this, that he lay down his life for his friends" (Jn 15:13).

Faith: "Suppose a brother or sister is without clothes and daily food. If one of you says to him, 'Go, I wish you well; keep warm and well fed,' but does nothing about his physical needs, what good is it?" (Jas 2:15-16).

The obvious remedy to ambiguity is to ask the other person to define his or her terms. Alice tried that with Humpty Dumpty.

"There's glory for you!"

"I don't know what you mean by 'glory,' " Alice said.

Humpty Dumpty smiled contemptuously. "Of course you don't—till I tell you. I meant 'there's a nice knockdown argument for you.' "

"But 'glory' doesn't mean 'a nice knockdown argument,' " Alice objected.

"When I use a word," Humpty Dumpty said, in a rather scornful tone, "it means just what I choose it to mean—neither more nor less."[5]

That seems to be stretching a word beyond the breaking point, but Humpty was not entirely wrong. Words don't mean things; people mean things. If we want to communicate our meaning accurately, we'd best define our terms.

More than once Jeanie and I have urged our kids to be *responsible*. Before long they dreaded the word. I'm not sure we ever spelled out what we had in mind, although there are lots of ways we might have put legs on it. Let's look at six.

We might resort to a dictionary. The chief rendering for responsible: "liable to be called on to answer."[6] Of course there's nothing verbally inspired about Webster's. All a dictionary attempts to do is reflect common usage. The Griffins are uncommon people. Perhaps our appeal to responsibility is to more than the possibility of being held answerable.

Sometimes it's helpful to look at a word's roots. *Responsible* = response + able = able to respond. That casts another light on the term. We might claim that our offspring will be able to respond if they get enough sleep at night. "You can't fly with the eagles in the morning if you hoot with the owls at night. Be responsible!"

Synonyms offer shorthand definitions. Disciplined. Diligent. Committed. None of these is less abstract than the original word, but together they help to explain it. Using another word with approximately the same thrust may not clear up all confusion, but it sure beats the ugly American's tendency merely to shout the same word louder.

Contrast is another way of clarifying. We don't always know what we want, but we're certain about what we hate. As the kids were growing up,

it would gall Jeanie if they slept in when there was work to be done. Responsibility was the opposite of laziness. Waiting till the last minute stirred my ire. I'd constantly harp on the pitfalls of not planning ahead. Responsibility meant not living for the moment. As parents we probably clarified by contrast much more than by declarative statements. Did our kids know what their folks wanted? I'm not sure. But there was no fuzziness over how to get a rise out of us.

Analogies use what is familiar to cast light on the unknown. Do we want to understand the concept of responsibility? The biting advice of Proverbs 6:6 is, "Go to the ant, O sluggard . . ." The continual labor, efficient organization and concern for the colony's welfare all illustrate the idea of human responsibility. Jesus' parables made the abstract kingdom of God easier to grasp. The miraculous raising of Lazarus and the feeding of the five thousand were living analogies of the Kingdom.

So far we've seen that we can define a word by resorting to a dictionary or by using etymology, synonyms, contrast and analogy. There's one other way, and it's my favorite—defining by example. Consider these effects:

"You took the responsibility to get your homework assignment when you were absent."

"She's a responsible girl. She always shows up when she says she'll be there."

"The height of being responsible is to stand up for a guy that's getting picked on."

This kind of concrete example may not make the dreaded word more palatable. But at least when it's served up the hearer will know the ingredients.

Not long ago I was asked to play referee in a conflict between two men in a Christian organization. They thought an outsider might bring objectivity to a deep-rooted dispute. The director acknowledged that the other guy was the best field worker in the mission but accused him of disloyalty. The staff member praised the director for his pastoral concern but said he couldn't respect the director because of his poor leadership. The first hour produced more heat than light. This was when I realized the gap was being widened by the abstract nature of the terms _disloyalty_ and _poor leadership_. I asked each man what he'd like the other man to do—specifically.

It took repeated probing, but each settled on three actions that could cause him to reverse his judgment. The director wanted the staff man to come to meetings on time, not to criticize his decisions publicly and to listen to a full explanation before raising questions. That would be loyalty. The field man wanted the director to pass information directly rather than through a secretary, not to waffle on a decision once it was made and to come see his work for a full day each quarter. That would be good leadership. When these desires were stated concretely, each realized he could give the other what he wanted. Clarity was the beginning of cooperation.

We think in pictures, not abstractions. That's why examples are effective in combating ambiguity. Billy Graham has noted that more people come forward when he speaks on the Christian life than when he preaches on sin or the cross. I think that's because the idea of becoming a Christian is a rather high-level abstraction. Analogies of marriage, being born again or setting Christ on the throne can help. But painting a verbal picture of how a Christian should live gives a secondhand reality that folks can try on for size. If it fits, they come forward.

Some communication scholars get bent out of shape bemoaning our sloppy use of language. They argue for precise word selection that leaves no wiggle room. To slightly alter the refrain of Dr. Seuss's Horton the

"Woah! Slow down, Mrs. Marney. Please keep in mind I have to translate all your laymen's terms into medical gobbledygook."

Elephant: I meant what I said, I said what I meant. A speaker's precise, one hundred per cent.[7]

The problem is that the word is not the thing. The relation of a word to the thing it refers to is like that of a map to the territory it depicts. The map is not the territory. It's merely a small-scale model that helps folks navigate a bit more easily. I have four different maps of Chicago. One shows all the expressway routes; it's great for cross-town planning. Another is a street map which shows every boulevard, road and cul de sac. With the accompanying index I can locate any address, but fully spread, this map blocks out my car's windshield. A Regional Transportation Authority map depicts bus, train and subway lines but is no good for driving. Finally, my aviation chart plots elevations, airports and radio navigation facilities. None of these is the *right* map of Chicago. They are different ways of describing the city—more or less helpful depending on what I want to do. No one map can do justice to the richness of the city. I need four—or more. Likewise, no one word can adequately convey the meaning a person gives to an object or idea. That's why paraphrasing is a good listening practice. It can bracket an idea with a number of similar expressions. This increases the possibility that two people can share a big hunk of the same meaning.

Paraphrasing is the art of restating, using new words, what you thought you heard. Let's try one. When Jesus talked with the woman at the well he said, "God is spirit, and his worshipers must worship in spirit and in truth" (Jn 4:24). It's possible to parrot back the same words to show you were listening. ("I hear you saying that God is spirit and those who worship him should do it in spirit and truth.") But that doesn't give the speaker any idea whether you caught his meaning. A real paraphrase would run something like this: "God is self-perpetuating. People who approach him must come in an authentic way with their whole being." I'm not at all sure this is what Jesus meant. I'd love to have the opportunity to discuss this passage with him, because it has always puzzled me. My attempt to restate what he said could open the door to further clarification. After four or five attempts to capture the essence of Jesus' words, I might have surrounded the meaning.

All this is not to say that word choice is a trivial matter. Winston Churchill altered the free world's image of the U.S.S.R. when he referred to Soviet isolation "behind the Iron Curtain." Or consider the College Board exams. Half of the student's score is based on language skill. The test makers assume that the ability to use words accurately is a clear reflection of mental sharpness. To the student who says, "I know what I think, I just can't put it into words," educators retort, _"Nonsense!"_—literally, "no sense."

But don't be misled. The clarity of shared meaning comes not from selecting the precise word, but from realizing how far short any word falls from describing reality. As a plaque on my wall states: "I know you believe you understand what you think I said, but I am not sure you realize that what you heard is not what I meant."

Perhaps the late Mayor Daley's press secretary wasn't the lousy communicator that reporters supposed. In exasperation he once blurted out, "They should have printed what he meant, not what he said."[8] All he was asking for was sensitive listeners.

Up to this point we've been talking about listening to language as if all we had to do was figure out the mental image standing behind a term. But language has connotation as well as denotation. Words _feel_ as well as point. The last section of this chapter will focus on times when understanding the affect is more important than picturing the referent.

How Words Feel

Imagine a college student at eight o'clock in the evening before a midterm exam. He has yet to crack a book. Instead he is camped in front of a TV set watching the World Series. What word do you think best describes the fellow in question? Your answer depends on how you feel about him, about baseball and about the importance of doing well on tests. Look at the six words in figure 4. All refer to the same guy watching the same game. But they run the gamut of emotional reaction. Note that I haven't inserted a word at the zero position. That's because I couldn't think of one that struck me as equally balanced between positive and negative. There aren't many neutral words in our vocabulary. We invest almost every one with feeling.

The wise listener quickly learns to identify the favorite emotionally loaded labels used by others. One communication scholar calls them God

Figure 4. Range of Emotional Meaning

Relaxed	Laid-back	Casual	Indifferent	Lazy	Slothful
+3	+2	+1	-1	-2	-3

terms and devil terms[9]—appropriate designations for Christian communicators. Right now *secular humanist* is a devil term for many Christians. To me, however, the label *humanist* can be quite positive. I tend to think of myself as a Christian humanist—one for whom Jesus is the ultimate example of what it means to be fully human. But no matter how I explain the word, if I use the term *humanist* I wave a red flag in front of many fellow Christians. Maybe to avoid creating the wrong impression I should stop referring to myself that way.

Sometimes the emotional warmth of conversation is the sum total of its message.

"Hi. How ya doin'?"

"Fine. How 'bout you?"

"Beautiful fall colors this time of year."

"Sure are. Nice to see you again."

"Thanks; you too."

In communication studies this is called *phatic communion,*[10] a label that has led one wag to refer to the above dialog as "chewing the phat." Many folks get impatient with its seemingly banal nature. They judge all communication by the amount of information it transmits. Lots of information that reduces the listener's uncertainty is good. A message devoid of content is bad. But that's missing the point of phatic communion. Its function is not to send information but to establish warm human contact. "I see you. I'm friendly. We're part of the same world." This is the implicit message. The conversation of two people in love often shares the same ritualistic function, but in this case the emotional loading of the words is more intense.

There's an interesting paradox at work here. People who are impatient with seemingly idle chatter often fail to achieve their goals. Their insistence on instrumental communication keeps them from establishing the warm ties that lubricate interactions and make them profitable. The art of small talk is a skill worth cultivating.

There's nothing trivial about listening to another share deeply felt emotions. Perhaps no other conversational activity offers such satisfying rewards. The talker gets a sympathetic sounding-board off which he can bounce his up-to-now private emotions. The listener gets to know another human being at a significantly deeper level. And the relationship takes a giant stride toward closeness. You'd think with such positive goodies in the offing we'd all become experts at this therapeutic type of listening. Unfortunately, most of us are only good at shutting off the self-disclosure tap.

Suppose a friend has just revealed that she feels angry at God because she is single. Take a look at the following listener responses, and see if you don't spot yourself.

"It's your own fault. You have such impossibly high standards that no man could possibly live up to them." We aren't usually this heavy-handed, but we often tell others their emotions are wrong. Nothing dries up the emotional well as quickly as *blame*.

"You're a big girl now. It's time you outgrew this adolescent romantic fantasy." This paternalistic advice can hurt more than the judgment of the first response. It suggests that any strong emotion is suspect for the mature adult. "Grow up" is the message of *shame*.

"I know exactly how you feel. I once felt God was against me when . . ." At first glance this may look like helpful identification with the woman who's hurting. But her feelings of anger and loneliness got lost in the shuffle. The listener has taken her feelings and staked his own *claim*.

"A feeling of alienation is a natural reaction to the growing phenomenon of urban isolation. It's understandable that you hold an omnipotent God responsible for your frustration." At best the person who shared feels as if she's being psychoanalyzed. At worst she feels like a bug under a microscope. I don't have a rhyming word to describe the clinical listeners. The closest I can come is *explain*.

"You say you feel mad at God, but I think you're overstating the case. You continue to tell others about Jesus and have regular devotions. You're

"You're always telling me you know exactly how I feel. Well, this time I'm calling your bluff. Exactly how *do* I feel?"

a model Christian." This flat-out denial of another's feelings is probably the cruelest cut of all. It's taking the other's words and making them null and void. I call it *maim*.

It was easy to write the five responses above. At one time or another I've mouthed every one of them. Why is it so hard to listen with an accepting ear? For me it may have to do with a desire for mastery or control. When others express strong hurts, I know I'm powerless to help them. I have no magic words to make life better. I hate the feeling of helplessness, so I blurt out one of these inappropriate responses to somehow get rid of the threat. It's the other guy who pays.

I do better when I relinquish the desire to fix people. When I'm not analyzing, admonishing or advocating I permit myself to hear the cries of their hearts. It's strange, but my attentive silence seems to be more helpful than my advice. What a blow to the ego. I'm in good company, though.

Psychologist Carl Rogers notes that unconditional acceptance frees clients so they can effectively draw upon self-healing resources.[11] In other words, they get better.

Rogers has another listening rule worth noting. He makes it a practice always to believe what the other person tells him. Other therapists laugh and call him naive. "Patients always lie," they claim. But Rogers holds firm. He trusts his patients because he believes trust is a healing balm.

Another clue to empathetic listening is to go light on probing questions. _Why_ questions are loaded with implied criticisms. As fascinated as we might be with another's motives, it's best to stick to asking for clarification of the present emotional state.

Here and Now.

I and Thou.

Not Why, but How.

Listening as an act of love is beautifully described by Tolstoy in _War and Peace_. It's a fitting close to this chapter on true listening, and it's an appropriate introduction to the next chapter on nonverbal communication:

Natasha, leaning on her elbow, the expression on her face continually changing with the story, watched Pierre, never taking her eyes off of him, and seemed to be experiencing with him all that he described. Not only her look but her exclamations and the brief questions she put showed Pierre that she understood just what he wanted to convey. It was clear that she understood not only what he said, but also what he would have liked to say but could not express in words.[12]

Pierre was a lucky man.

6
NONVERBAL COMMUNICATION

You cannot not communicate.

THE MEMORY IS SEARED into my brain. On a beautiful fall football afternoon, as thousands were streaming toward the University of Michigan stadium, I caught a glimpse of Maxine Rupachevski—with another guy, Bob. I managed to get within twenty feet of them for about a minute before they were lost in the swirl of people. It was more than enough time to convince me that Maxine Rupachevski wasn't going to simplify her name by changing it to Griffin.

I couldn't distinguish a single word they said to each other, but I was able to pick up a host of nonverbal cues which left no doubt as to the nature of their relationship. The fact that Maxine didn't intend to communicate this information to me made no difference. Her behavior was open to public scrutiny, and I got the message. She was probably not thinking about this principle of communication that fall afternoon, but she illustrated it nevertheless: You cannot not communicate.

Nonverbal communication includes all the nonlinguistic things a person does to which others ascribe meaning. Nonverbal signals are particularly effective in communicating feelings toward others. One researcher claims that ninety-three per cent of the emotional dynamics in a relationship are conveyed through facial expressions and tone of voice, and only seven per cent through actual words.[1] I might quibble about the exact ratio, but I agree that nonverbal channels tell us most of what we know about an interpersonal relationship.

There are three main dimensions that define the relationship between two people—attraction, arousal and power.[2] As in a three-ring circus, what's going on in one ring is separate from the activities in the other two, but you need to scan all three acts to get a handle on the entire show. I didn't have to be a prophet to read the nonverbal signals in the three arenas of Maxine and Bob's relationship.

Attraction has to do with distance. We approach things we like; we avoid things that cause displeasure. Maxine took pleasure in Bob's company. In the first place they were together—voluntarily. They walked close together, bumping "accidentally" as they went along. They held eye contact repeatedly—quite tricky to do while moving. Just before I lost sight of them I was dealt the ultimate blow. They reached out and held hands. Close interpersonal distance, mutual gaze, touch—all signs of intimacy.

Arousal is marked by change. A flat tone of voice and a single expression on the face would signal lack of interest. What I saw was the exact opposite. Maxine's face was animated by dozens of different expressions during the few moments I observed her. The lilt of her voice flowing like waves over the crowd noise revealed a heightened awareness of her partner. Fortunately, I wasn't close enough to observe whether or not the pupils of her eyes were enlarged—another indicator that the sympathetic nervous system is working overtime. (Pupil dilation is also one danger sign of concussion—just what I was feeling.)

Power is a dirty word to a lot of folks, especially when it is applied to interpersonal relationships. But no communication takes place apart from questions of status. In fact, there's a whole field of discourse analysis that categorizes messages on a dominant-submissive scale.[3] "One up" messages assume superiority, whereas "one down" utterances grant it to the other.

The nonverbal signals I saw between Maxine and Bob reflected a "one across" equality, a parity of power. Relative status is often evidenced in body posture—the comfortably relaxed superior in contrast to the tense subordinate. Bob and Maxine were equally relaxed as they strolled with the crowd. Their jeans-and-sweater attire showed a mutuality of comfort. There were no signs of possession or territoriality as they passed a jug of sweet apple cider back and forth. The crowning blow came when they each took a pull without bothering to wipe off the rim, hinting of germs comingled in the past.

Figure 5 charts what I saw that fateful day. Each of the three dimensions is necessary to define the relationship. Together they say it all. In the jargon of academia, they are a "necessary and sufficient explanation of the phenomena." In my heart of hearts, I was devastated.

Figure 5. Defining a Relationship

	Attraction	
Approach X		Avoidance

	Arousal	
Responsiveness X		Nonresponsive

	Power	
High Status	X	Low Status

(Xs indicate perceived relationship between Maxine and Bob.)

I imagined that Bob and Maxine's conversation paralleled the warmth, responsiveness and mutuality I observed in their actions. Suppose I had a transcript of their actual words and discovered that they were speaking of the Russian invasion of Czechoslovakia, the devaluation of the dollar or methods of group Bible study—nonpersonal topics with no apparent bearing on their relationship. Would I have found that reassuring? Would I have taken heart, thinking they weren't as close as the nonverbal signs suggested? Not likely. When there's dissonance between the words we hear and the nonverbal cues surrounding them, we usually believe the extralinguistic data.[4] "Seeing is believing."

How come? I think it has to do with deception. Most folks figure it's harder to lie with the body than with words. We pick up this idea early— perhaps because we know how people are responding to us well before we can understand what they are saying. Think of an Old Western film where one man in the saloon is called a cattle rustler. "Smile when you say that, pardner," is his response, and the other man's life hangs in the balance. The cowboy is willing to judge whether the words are a slur to his manhood or merely rough-and-tumble humor, based on whether the speaker's mouth is turned up in a smile or down in a sneer. Nonverbal communication is the punctuation that tells us how to interpret words; thus it is the final arbiter of our relationships.[5]

© Punch—ROTHCO

"We're looking for someone who can lie convincingly. The hard part is knowing when we've found him!"

Some kids get caught in a "double bind" with their parents. This term used by family therapists describes the dilemma a child faces when the parents say one thing but convey another through facial expression and tone of voice. "I'd love to go to your piano recital," says the kid's father, but his hurried manner, pained expression and sarcastic inflection give his words the lie. If his son or daughter plaintively responds to the mood that came across, the dad takes refuge in the words. "I said I want to go to the concert. Can't you understand English?" But kids aren't fooled by this "crazy-making" ploy. They instinctively know it's harder to lie nonverbally than with words.

Of course some people get good at it. An effective confidence man, actor or impersonator is successful precisely because he has learned the art of nonverbal impression management. But when push comes to shove, we'll usually resolve a contradiction between words and how they're said by giving the nod to the nonverbal signs. In most cases it's a wise choice.

Having shared my grief on that long-ago football afternoon in order to show the important place of nonverbal communication, I'd like to leave Maxine and Bob and take a closer look at research findings concerning body movement, eye contact, tone of voice, touch, and so on. Some researchers label these respective fields *kinesics, proxemics, vocalics* and *haptics*. This shows their belief that nonverbal communication is a parallel system to linguistics with a lexicon, syntax and semantic rules. I'm not convinced, and the terms have a rather stodgy tone. So I'll stick with labels we all understand. The student of the field who wants to investigate further can check the end notes for the accepted academic labels and major sources of research.

Gestures[6]

Gestures are any kind of body movement from the neck down. (Facial expression and eye behavior are special breeds, so I'll treat them separately.) Gestures serve at least five different functions. Understanding them won't automatically improve your one-on-one communication, but it will give you a greater awareness of the wealth of data coming through the nonverbal channel.

Emblems are nonverbal substitutes for words. The hitchhiker's thumb means, "I'd like a ride." A shoulder shrug with open palms in response to a question means, "I don't know." The A-OK symbol of thumb and forefinger forming a circle means, "Things are good." This body language is just as culture bound as its linguistic equivalent. There are few if any universal gestures.

The symbol that means "A-OK" in America is a reference to money in the Philippines. A group of dirt-poor farmers once showed me the account books for their cooperative. Not knowing Tagalog, I tried to use that thumb-index gesture to indicate my approval of their efforts. They read it as a sarcastic commentary on their finances.

When Richard Nixon traveled to Latin America as vice president he got off the plane and made the same gesture as a way of indicating solidarity with the people. The gesture was featured on TV and in the press, and he later experienced an angry mob throwing rocks at his limousine. That reaction doesn't seem totally unreasonable when we understand that to Latins the thumb-index circle is an obscene gesture similar to our giving someone the finger.

Most cultures have a lexicon of one hundred to two hundred emblems. Since these aren't usually taught in a foreign language class, international travelers would be wise to check with someone who is visually bilingual to make sure they aren't offending with their gestures.

Illustrators are gestures that give a picture of what the speaker is saying. "The fish was two feet long, honest."

"The school is right down this road—you can't miss it."

"The kitten dove into the bag; it was so cute!"

"When you put the right aileron down, the plane banks to the left."

These statements scream out for nonverbal clarification. Of course to communicate effectively, the words and the body picture must match. Go to a football game and you'll undoubtedly see cheerleaders imploring the crowd to "Lean to the left. Lean to the right. Stand up. Sit down. Fight, fight, fight!" The cheer usually fails to stimulate the crowd to unified action. I think that's because there's dissonance between the words and the motions. When the cheerleaders shout "Lean to the left," they follow their own advice. But that's _their_ left. From the crowd's perspective their body tilt is to the right, which doesn't square with the directions. Once I saw a cheerleading team reverse their action so as to reinforce their words. Their nonverbal communication was effective.

Affect display is a revelation of emotion, whether overt or subtle. We have no doubt about how people feel if they shake their fists in anger or jump for joy. Often the disclosure is more restrained. Arms folded across the chest may reflect guardedness. Legs propped on a desk can signal an overall sense of comfort. I once had a heavyweight wrestler in a night class who sat sprawled in a back-row chair. He wore mirror sun glasses and his face was a total mask, so I got no feedback about his feelings. The only indication of life within was his rhythmic squeezing of a rubber ball in his left hand—presumably to strengthen his grip. I'd just about given up having any impact on the guy when I noticed that during one of my better illustrations he briefly stopped squeezing the ball. It wasn't much, but it was all I had. I soon learned to gauge his interest level by the length of time he'd quit worrying the ball. Each week I'd come home and tell Jeanie how many times he had paused. ("It was a five-stopper tonight.") One night when I was really clicking he became so absorbed that the ball rolled out of his palm—total victory for me. (I hope it didn't cost him the match.)

Regulators are motions that guide the flow of communication. Like traffic cops, these gestures indicate whose turn it is to go ahead. An upraised hand requests permission to speak. Pointing at the petitioner grants it. Body leaning forward says, "I'm ready to hear you." Body leaning back says, "I'm not." Sweeping gestures during a verbal pause shows I'm not ready to relinquish the floor.

We can't look at regulating gestures in isolation. They blend with other nonverbal signals like eye contact and tone of voice to orchestrate a total impression. Just as paragraphing and punctuation help bring order out of the chaos on the printed page, nonverbal regulators help folks work out a turn-taking ritual so not everyone is speaking at once.

Adaptors are semiconscious motions, usually rooted in childhood, that help us cope with the world. Some people scratch their heads. Others bite their fingernails, crack their knuckles or rub the back of their necks. For years when seated in a chair I jiggled my right leg up and down about two hundred forty cycles per minute. It was as if the limb had a life of its own. Fidgeting mannerisms aren't intended for public consumption. Rather they spring up as an outlet for inner tension. Not surprisingly, however, the naive psychologist in all of us almost always picks them up in other people. Lots of times these distracting movements slough off as we become comfortable with who we are. That removes some static from the channel.

Facial Display[7]
What's the girl on page 121 feeling? Take a few seconds and jot down the emotions you pick up from her six different facial expressions.[8]

1. *Happiness.* Whether the emotion is joy, amusement, satisfaction or love, the telltale sign of happiness is in the lower third of the face. The mouth and cheeks crinkle up to show pleasure. That doesn't mean the eyes and forehead don't come into play. It's just that the happy action is in the mouth.

2. *Sadness.* Sadness shows most in the eyebrows and forehead— the upper third of the face. Whether it's passive melancholy or active distress, the wrinkled brow is the characteristic sign of sadness.

3. *Disgust.* This reaction could be mistaken for anger were it not for the mouth. When a person feels revulsion the lips form an uneven line.

4. *Fear.* Fear differs from sadness in that the eyes open wide when a person is frightened. You'll seldom see fear displayed on a male face. Social convention says men don't show fear in public.

5. *Anger.* From minor annoyance to rage, anger is etched on the face with a tightly clenched mouth and arched brow. Just as men don't show fear in public, most women observe an unwritten rule by not letting on when they're mad.

6. *Surprise.* Surprise shows on the entire facial map. Eyebrows are extended upward, the eyes are round, and the mouth drops open. Perhaps because of the multiple indicators, surprise is rarely misconstrued.

Figure 6. Six Facial Displays

How did you do? My guess is quite well. Most folks nail all six emotions. That may be because these expressions seem to transcend cultural boundaries. A New Guinea tribesman who has never seen a Caucasian in person or a photograph can look at these pictures and identify the feelings. Copycat empathy is a possible explanation for the universal recognition of facial display. We see another's reactions and our facial muscles automatically mirror the same look. Knowing how the expression feels, we can then identify the mood that goes with it.

Over fifty per cent of emotional meaning is picked up from facial expression. Most people are pretty good at reading faces, though some are better than others. Women usually decode more accurately than men. Counselors and others in people-helping professions often master the skill. They learn to zero in on different areas of the face to pick up separate emotions. Figure 6 gives the answers with the display clues that are dead giveaways to the feelings.

These symbolic drawings and simplistic descriptions suggest that facial expression are uniform displays of single emotions. That's often not the case. There is more channel capacity in the face than in any other nonverbal mode. Complex blends of affects are typical. When people want to shield an emotion from public view they usually send mixed signals. It's easier to inhibit or mute an expression than to lie visually. A "poker face" conceals much of the natural muscle response, but leakage occurs in one way or another. Slow-motion films of people in unnatural situations often reveal fleeting looks of anger, fear or disgust sandwiched between two

"That was unkind, darling. When their mouths turn up at the corners they want to be friends."

smiles. These looks are too quick to note consciously, but they may well register subliminally. Or the right side of the face may show pleasure while the left side reveals a negative emotion. I think we can usually trust our instincts. If a person strikes us as mad, she probably is.

Eye Behavior[9]

The eye is the "window of the soul." I once heard a Christian leader claim he could tell if a girl was sexually immoral just by looking in her eyes. He seemed not to be bothered by the arrogance of the claim, the potential harm he could do by his judgment or the possibility that his conclusions might reflect more his desire than the girl's character. Most of us are more restrained in our claims to interpret eye behavior, but our language is filled with stock phrases showing confidence in the ability to read the inner person through the eyes: an icy stare, a gleam in her eye, a bold glance, the evil eye, shifty eyes, eyes brimming with happiness, laughing eyes.

All these terms attribute personality traits or emotional moods to people based on their eye behavior alone. As you saw in the facial test, eyes show only part of what a person is feeling. But some communication factors can be picked up by watching just the eyes. Channel control is one.

Eye contact signals that both parties are ready to communicate. The pipeline is open; the spigot's turned on. Mutual gaze implies an obligation to interact; so if we don't want to talk, we avoid eye contact. The patron in the crowded restaurant tries to catch the waitress's eye. But she has three more tables to serve before she responds to the ocular request, so she carefully avoids looking over. The teacher asks a question over an assigned reading no one has done. Instantly the room is like a prayer meeting—every head bowed, every eye shut. No one wants to risk getting called on by making eye contact with the prof. And most folks shut their eyes during group prayer because they want to communicate with God. Mutual gaze would put the emphasis on human relationships and would distract from the stated purpose.

We also avoid eye contact if we're doing some heavy-duty thinking. Suppose I ask you what 12 x 13 equals or which eight states border on

Tennessee. You'll invariably break eye contact and look to the side. Cognitive activity and eye contact are extremely difficult to maintain at the same time. That's one good reason for public speakers to know their material well—if they're having to grope for their next point, their gaze will wander, and audiences get turned off fast by speakers who won't look at them. There's even some evidence of systematic differences between people who gaze to the left and those who avert their eyes to the right. Consistent with research on dominant hemispheres of the brain, left-lookers tend to be more musical, religious, interested in the humanities and susceptible to hypnosis. They do better on the verbal part of College Board exams. Right-lookers seem to be more interested in science, more likely to make career choices earlier in life and more tense. They do better on the math part of aptitude tests.

I wouldn't want to stake my life's savings on these findings, but we often make crucial decisions based on direction of gaze. Lowered eyes speak of modesty. Most of us implicitly believe someone is telling the truth if he tells his story looking us straight in the eye. As a matter of fact, there is some evidence that deceit and shifting gaze do go together. But that doesn't automatically mean the person with the level gaze is telling the truth. Some folks get good at lying while looking you straight in the eye.

Up to this point I've concentrated on direction of gaze. Now let's look at duration. As with many things in life, appropriateness is in the middle range. Holding eye contact for too brief a time can make us look either furtive or bored. A normal amount of direct gaze shows interest. Too much eye contact and the other person begins to squirm. In a two-person conversation it's typical to look at the other person forty per cent of the time while speaking, seventy per cent of the time while listening. But I find that seventy per cent is too long when I'm listening to students in my office. With my deep-set brown eyes and bushy eyebrows, anything over thirty seconds feels like laser beams burning holes into them. To avoid making them uncomfortable with that intensity, I work at looking away. My children, Jim and Sharon, have grown up with my prolonged, searching gaze. They've labeled it "The Look," and they are quick to add that they don't like it.

A constant stare communicates coldness at best, an angry challenge at worst. The first time I formally studied nonverbal communication was at Northwestern University's graduate school. Every afternoon after classes I took the elevated train from Evanston to Chicago. At one place there are parallel tracks, and it's possible for two trains to travel side by side at forty miles per hour. You can be hurtling along only eighteen inches away from another person.

After a seminar session on eye contact I decided to test the effect of staring at the person opposite me on the other El train. I promised myself I wouldn't avert my gaze as long as the trains stayed together. As luck would have it, the guy alongside me looked fierce, complete with cycle jacket and shaved head. After thirty seconds of my unswerving gaze he opened the window and shook his fist at me—brass knuckles and all. I was grateful the trains didn't stop at the same station and concluded that one demonstration in the cause of science was quite sufficient.

I remember Secretary of State Dean Rusk's famous report at the time of the Cuban missile crisis. After issuing an ultimatum to Andrei Gromyko, the Soviet foreign minister, he reported: "We're eyeball to eyeball, . . . and I think the other guy just blinked." If you're going to stare, you'd better be prepared to play hardball.

Pupil dilation is a lesser-known but equally fascinating part of reading eyes. Of course the eye opens or closes to adjust to the external light available. But pupil size has also been used to infer internal responses. Early research hinted that enlarged pupils meant attraction to the person or object being seen. ("The kid pressed his nose against the toy store window, his eyes as big as saucers.")

Dilated pupils are often interpreted as romantic interest, as you'll see in the next chapter. Recent findings, however, indicate that attraction is only one possible explanation. Pupil enlargement, it seems, is linked to any strong emotion. Whether the system is turned on by fear, surprise, anger, sexual arousal or happiness—the pupils expand. (Recall the image of children listening wide-eyed to a ghost story.) Without other signals to clarify what other people are feeling, all we can say for sure is that they are not feeling bored.

"Wait a minute! You mean everybody here is a wolf!"

Appearance[10]

I came home last night and met a guy with a two-day growth of beard. He was dressed in a wrinkled pullover and faded jeans frayed at the bottom, and he wore one earring in a pierced left lobe. This morning I was greeted by a clean-shaven young man looking smart in a dress shirt, tie and polished shoes. He was wearing no jewelry. It was the same fellow—my son, Jim.

Some things are written in stone. Short of plastic surgery, the shape of my nose is a given. My skin color can be altered only within a narrow range. But it's amazing how much of my self- presentation can come under my conscious control. That's especially true in how I dress.

Clothes make the man.

That's the message of *Gentlemen's Quarterly*, and it's echoed on the female side by *Vogue, Seventeen* and a legion of copycat periodicals. The Salvation Army just hauled away an old leisure suit and a pair of polyester slacks that didn't quite touch my feet. To wear them would be to make a statement I don't want to make. Style of dress can send a message just as

"Just once I'd like to see a diet-cola commercial with a girl who really needs a diet cola!"

loudly as a T-shirt proclaiming "One Way," "I'd rather be skiing" or "Save the whales." The message is muted when a person's dress style blends in with that of others in the same situation. Appropriateness and approval are kissing cousins when it comes to clothing. The more someone departs from the norm, the more he demands, "Pay attention to me." We do—but usually don't like what we see.

Hair is crucial to self-presentation. For fifteen years I sported a Lincoln-esque beard. As I'd visit an inner-city housing project all the kids would shout, "Hey, Abe!" (Except for one guy who called me George. He knew I looked like a president, but he wasn't quite sure which one.) Because of my Lincoln look, many of these folks attributed liberal social views to me. (True.) My students at school, noting that it was neatly trimmed, would assume I am an organized, meticulous person. (False!) Since I shaved it off, most folks tell me I look ten years younger. If I had taken the hair off the top of my head rather than off my chin, they'd be adding years rather than subtracting them.

Some people get offended when others jump to conclusions because of their clothes or hair style. They think it's unfair to stereotype people by their outward appearance. "Look at the real me," they protest. But visual stereotypes typically become widespread only when they have some basis in reality. It's not unreasonable to assume that people select a look or style because they want to identify with what it represents. I'm not defending knee-jerk responses. Anytime we start a sentence with the word _all,_ we're in trouble. I am suggesting, however, that we select our nonverbal statements—including our personal appearance—as carefully as we choose our words. Both say a lot about us.

One area of appearance in which we have less choice is body shape. Although we can affect muscle tone through exercise, and weight through diet, we can't control our natural height or bone structure. Early efforts in psychology tried to establish a link between body type and personality. As modern sophisticates, we smile at the naive notion that fat people are automatically jolly, or thin folks naturally shy. But ongoing research suggests we shouldn't laugh too quickly. Take a look at the three body outlines on page 131.

People who approximate one of these three basic shapes tend to describe themselves in similar words.[11] How come? Does body structure influence disposition? Do people assume that personality traits go with physical appearance, and thus a self-fulfilling prophecy takes place? Or does inner attitude affect the way we eat and exercise? My guess is all three are true. One thing is certain—when people think they can "read us like a book," they're taking into account the dimensions of the cover, strength of the binding, and overall thickness. Lots of books have gone unread because they appeared too dense.

Use of Space[12]
For the last fifteen years I've been landing an airplane on an island in Lake Michigan. A flock of three hundred sea gulls takes flight whenever they hear the sound of my engine. You'd think they'd keep their distance—after all, I'm a bigger bird and I make more racket. Yet every time I'm on final approach or climbing out on take-off they swirl in front of the plane in

Figure 7. Three Body Types

Endomorphic: soft, round, fat	Mesomorphic: bony, muscular, athletic	Ectomorphic: tall, thin, fragile
dependent	dominant	detached
calm	cheerful	tense
relaxed	confident	anxious
complacent	energetic	reticent
contented	impetuous	self-conscious
sluggish	efficient	meticulous
placid	enthusiastic	reflective
leisurely	competitive	precise
cooperative	determined	thoughtful
affable	outgoing	considerate
tolerant	argumentative	shy
affected	talkative	awkward
warm	active	cool
forgiving	domineering	suspicious
sympathetic	courageous	introspective
soft-hearted	enterprising	serious
generous	adventurous	cautious
affectionate	reckless	tactful
kind	assertive	sensitive
sociable	optimistic	withdrawn
soft-tempered	hot-tempered	gentle-tempered

a frenzied pattern that's both beautiful and frightening. It seems inevitable that we'd mash together, but at the last second they dive downward, slip to the side or soar above my path.

Until this summer. In the space of a week, I had two different strikes, one on the windshield, the other close in on the wing. These were not glancing blows but head-on collisions causing significant damage. The

Drawing by Peter Steiner. Reprinted with permission.

direct frontal nature of the crashes suggested that the gulls were attacking the plane in a desperate one-on-one contest. After fifteen years of seemingly peaceful coexistence, why now?

According to the Department of Natural Resources, the key issue is probably the location of the sea gull nests. Despite my clear title to the land, the gulls have always regarded me as an intruder. When their nests were off to the side of the runway, I was an irritant. They took flight, put up a squawk, then flew away. But gradually over the years the nesting area has crept closer to the runway. I've had to take care not to disturb the eggs when I've mowed the grass. The gulls now see my glide path as a menace to their lives. I've moved from flight distance to fight distance. In a heroic effort to protect their young, they've taken on the iron bird.

Naturalists call this phenomenon _territoriality_—an animal's effort to stake out its own turf. Human animals do the same thing. A housewife's kitchen, a father's chair, a teen-ager's bedroom are special private places. Trespass at your own risk. We use all sorts of not-so-subtle strategies to let others know the boundaries of our space. Banging pots and pans in frantic activity, leaving a book or article of clothing on the seat of the chair, closing (even slamming) the door—all proclaim, "This place is mine."

If we let someone else invade space we've carved out for ourselves, it means either high attraction or low power. A desire for affiliation with another can overcome our demand for privacy. I remember an InterVarsity camp that scheduled forty-five minutes each morning for a quiet time. The first day I discovered a big boulder that afforded support for my back and a view of the water. The second day I dashed there, hoping no one else had discovered it. By the third morning I figured it was mine. Toward the end of the week I arrived to discover that someone had usurped my rock. But she was pretty and pleasant, so I didn't object. For a while it became "our" rock.

Another invasion occurred a few days later. As I came into the clearing I saw size-twelve boots, a clear sign that the interloper was male. I was just preparing to assert my prior claim to the territory when the whole man came into view. It was the camp speaker. I'm sure he would have moved if I had raised a fuss, but rank has its privileges. I grudgingly saw his higher status as sufficient reason to let him have access to my territory. A high-power person can enter my space because I feel I can't keep him out. A highly attractive person can enter because I want her in. It's easy for an outsider to miss the distinction.

So far I've treated distance as an either/or, in/out deal. Actually it's more like a sliding scale. Edward Hall identifies four ranges depending on the kind of transaction that's going on. _Intimate_ distance is from zero to eighteen inches. Touch, body heat and odor are ways we gauge the exact space between us. *Personal* distance is from eighteen inches to four feet. It's the normal friendship range. While touch is still possible and strong smells come into play, the eyes and ears are the main way to sense appropriate space. *Social* distance runs from four to twelve feet. Visual and aural means are used to monitor space. Party talk, business discussions in an office and sales in a store usually take place within this category. *Public* distance discourages dialog. One-way communication is typical from twelve feet on out. When students avoid front-row seats in a classroom, they're defining the situation as one of formal interaction rather than mutual exchange— and they're probably right.

I wouldn't quibble if you wanted to adjust Hall's figures one way or another. He did his research on only six people in the northeastern United States, one of them Erich Fromm's wife. (Not exactly a random sample of humanity.) Hall himself takes pains to point out that different cultures have different standards for what is considered appropriate distance in a given situation. This can cause misunderstandings in international business and diplomatic transactions. Imagine the plight of the English businessman as his personal space is invaded by a "pushy" Arab who's continually advancing too close for comfort. Imagine the frustration the Arab feels as that "cold" Briton retreats. How can he be trusted if he denies the Arab the smell of his breath?

Culture and relationship aren't the only variables that affect interpersonal distance. Architecture can have a major impact. For years banks were designed to create the impression of power and permanence at the cost of warmth. Many potential customers opted for "friendly Bob Adams" in the cozy office of Household Finance at double the interest rate. The conversational grouping in the family room or den promotes intimacy, whereas the distances in the un-living room dictate that it be kept for formal occasions. Averting eyes has the effect of making close distances seem farther away. It's tolerable to stand in an elevator or sit in a theater at intimate distance from a stranger as long as both people have their gaze fixed on something else. Let one person look at the other and the psychological distance between them telescopes uncomfortably.

Put all these factors together and one truth holds sway: As we talk with someone else there's a distance that seems just right. What happens if the other person comes too close? Nothing if it's only a minor discrepancy— we can live with it. But once she or he crosses the threshold of appropriateness we can feel the juices flow. Our heart rate goes up, the adrenalin pumps, our palms sweat, our muscles tense. All these are signs that the central nervous system is turned on. That will be pleasant if the person entering our bubble is highly attractive to us. But the experience will be unpleasant if we have any reservations about the person's desirability. If he has irritated us before, as a space invader he will seem insufferable. If you aren't sure how you stand with another, don't bash into his or her bubble of space. When in doubt, stay out.

Touch[13]

Touch is special to me. As I write this with my right hand, my left hand is stroking a soft, white, purring kitten curled on my lap. She can get to me in ten seconds flat. Tonight I go to the YMCA where a student from the nearby chiropractic college will give me a thirty-minute massage of my back, neck, arms and feet. My friends know I'm always up for a hug. I recently read an essay claiming that the only forms of touch legitimate in American culture are shaking hands, fighting and making love.[14] If I were limited to these forms of tactile expression, I think I'd quickly shrivel up and waste away.

Many communication researchers treat touch as a type of distance—a zero space between two people. That's not how most "real" people react. They see touch as a whole new ball game, different from distance in kind as well as degree. For one thing, those central nervous system indicators we talked about in the last section take a quantum leap when tactile contact is made. For another, touch has many separate nuances depending on what part of the body is touched and what part does the touching, the length of time the touch lasts, the amount of pressure applied, the type of movement involved, whether anyone else is present, and the relationship between the pair. No tactile lexicon can honestly state that a given touch has a certain meaning.

With that caution in mind, let me list a few of the findings of tactile communication research.

☐ The person initiating touch has the higher status. The coach puts his arm around the player's shoulder—not the other way around. When a man touches a woman, he may regard it as a sign of affection. She may interpret it as a power play to keep her in a submissive role.

☐ Mixed sex pairs touch more than same-sex friends. Male pairs are less comfortable with mutual touch than females. I've seen this over and over at camp. Assign two girls to sleep in a double bed and it's OK. Tell two guys to share a bed and they die in a pile.

☐ Touch is an intensifier. If those I like reach out to touch me, I'll like them more. If I have even a mild aversion to them, skin contact will make me cringe and I'll start working on a genuine hate. Once on a retreat I assigned pairs to spend time walking together. An attractive girl reached out and took the arm of the guy she was with. "I'll give you thirty minutes to cut that out," was his pleased response. It was the start of something long-term.

Voice[15]

Jennifer was a former teaching assistant and student of mine. For a while after graduation we stayed in touch by mail and phone. Two years ago her phone was disconnected—"No further information available." Two or three of my letters went unanswered. I was stymied until last week, when I heard she was living in a small town two thousand miles away. I was able to get a number from directory assistance, and I took the plunge. A female voice answered.

"Jennifer . . . ?" was all I said.

"Em!" she exclaimed and launched off on a ten-minute review of the past twenty-four months.

One word was all she needed. The sound of a person's voice is as unique as a fingerprint or a signature. Claims for graphology notwithstanding, we can tell a lot more about a person from vocal clues than from handwriting. Consider your own telephone experience. It's usually no problem knowing the sex of the caller. Age, body size, race, education, and geographical origin can be figured out with reasonable accuracy. Even with the static of a bad connection you can identify the other's mood. Jennifer told me I sounded warm when I said her name, so she knew she didn't have to feel guilty for dropping out of touch.

That's a pretty big load to place on the vocal channel, but it can carry the weight. Perhaps it's because there are so many ways to vary the voice—volume, speed, pitch and tone are just a few.

We tend to equate high *volume* with power. Fighting words are loud. So are the orders of a drill sergeant or football coach. Soft words come from subordinates or equals. They also turn away wrath. Early in my speaking career I spoke six times in three days at a Bible college. Afterward a student pulled me aside and said almost accusingly, "You've moved people: I want to know how you did it." Seeing my confusion he went on, "You've had an impact, yet you never once yelled at us." Based on his experience with chapel speakers this seemed incongruous. They'd presented the power of the gospel with a powerful voice. Many of today's TV preachers take the same strident approach. But I didn't want my listeners to feel inferior or guilty, so I chose a "let us reason together" level that seemed to strike a responsive chord.

The world is not fair. Normal human speaking *pitch* ranges over two octaves, and we react differently to the upper and lower registers. A high voice conjures up the image of a person who is flighty, shallow and tense. Only the tension has any basis in reality: muscle tension can pull the vocal cords taut—just like tightening a guitar string—and raise the speaking pitch about four notes. Low pitch projects stability and sincerity. Deep and husky is preferred over light and airy at auditions for radio announcers. As I said, it's not a fair world.

When it comes to *rate* of speech, it's hard to separate the good guys from the ones in the black hats. In general, our culture sees slow, halting speech as a sign of ignorance, shyness or complacency. A faster pace usually strikes folks as more attractive, alive and powerful. But not always. Quickness of tongue can also be seen as fast-talking wheeling-dealing or just being a motor mouth. The difficulty arises not so much from the speed at which an idea is presented, but from a lack of pauses. Breaks in the action are nonverbal invitations for others to comment. If a person plows straight through or fills the pauses with "and," "you know" and "uh," listeners conclude they're merely witnesses to monolog rather than partners in dialog. And they're right.

Tone is a catch-all term to describe a voice's quality. It's hard to say anything intelligent about tone of voice without using recorded examples. I'll only point out that some traditionally recognized tone patterns may give others an unwanted impression. A monotone, devoid of inflection, signals the listener that everything's a pain, everyone a bore.

I once greeted a girl on campus with a wave and a, "How's it going?"

"It's a long story," she sighed, and her flat tone gave me the feeling that I didn't want to hear it.

The ministerial tone gets soft and breathy every time the speaker refers to "G . . . a . . . h . . . d." That passes for reverence but conjures up the idea of a Creator who is comfortable only when surrounded by stained glass. A nasal twang can set others on edge. Vitamin C or hay-fever pills might help avoid the resulting interpersonal tension. Resonance is attractive, but a person talking one-on-one as if she were addressing a large throng strikes a pompous note. I was recently on the receiving end of an orotund utterance: "The franchise restaurants are ubiquitous on this road." The devil in me responded, "There are lots of fast food places too."

When you add the sounds of gushy sentimentality, the precious lilt associated with some homosexuals, or the timorous quake of a fearful petitioner, a guy could get the idea that it's best never to open his mouth. But that's neither possible nor desirable. The key to avoiding pitfalls is to work on variety. If the tone matches the words, people will get the right idea.

Smell[16]

Odor has the power to access our deepest feelings. The smell of chlorine invariably tightens my stomach as it calls up memories of high-school swimming competitions. I instantly associate a whiff of rough-cut cedar with feelings of warmth and love. Realtors instruct folks that the smell of baking bread or boiling apples can transform their house into a home.

For Americans, most bodily smells are negative. The aromas of soap,

"I want to impress a special boy. Got any perfume that smells like the slime monster from outer space?"

antiseptic, mint or hair spray have come to seem more "natural" than the real thing. None of us know for sure how we smell to others. The only advice I have is to occasionally ask and always listen.

That's not a bad note on which to close this chapter. Most of us are not trained in nonverbal communication. Our repertoire of symbols we know how to use is smaller than our rich collection of reactions toward others. It's possible that the signals we think we're sending are being picked up as something quite different. Soliciting verbal feedback on our nonverbal behavior is wise relational insurance. We may not like the emotional cost of the premium, but it's a small price to pay for avoiding interpersonal disaster.

7
INTERPERSONAL ATTRACTION

Without identification,
there is no communication.

IN THE LAST CHAPTER we saw how to tell if people are attracted to us—
or how to communicate that we enjoy them. In this chapter we'll look at
why people like each other. Some say this is a fool's errand. They think
friendship is triggered by an interpersonal chemistry that can't be ex-
plained. It's ruled by sheer luck. But I'm not satisfied with that. Even the
casual observer of the human scene is able to spot some apparent patterns
of attraction. A number of maxims have surfaced through the years. Here's
a partial list:

A friend in need is a friend indeed.

Misery loves company.

Absence makes the heart grow fonder.

Familiarity breeds contempt.

Out of sight, out of mind.

Pray together, stay together.

Everybody loves a winner.

Politics makes strange bedfellows.

Birds of a feather flock together.

Opposites attract.

If you want a friend, be a friend.

Love is blind.

The best way to lose a friend is to lend him money.

These age-old sayings contain popular wisdom that seems self-evident. Some of these "truths," however, are diametrically opposed. "Birds of a feather . . . ," for example, contradicts "Opposites attract." Which is true? Obviously there's a problem with relying on the obvious.

There's no need to despair. Social researchers have worked hard in the past few decades to sort out the causes of attraction. While they haven't achieved anything close to one hundred per cent predictability, certain patterns have emerged.

Friendship is a personal subject, so I want to make this as personal as possible. I'll use my relationship with a close friend to illustrate the findings on interpersonal attraction. I'd like you to do the same—pick a close or intimate friend, and keep this person in mind as you read. As I suggest factors that draw people together, see if they fit your situation. My guess is that most of them will.

Intimacy isn't an either/or proposition. As figure 8 shows, there's a sliding scale that starts with "mere acquaintance" on one end and moves toward "intimate friend" on the other. The position of the steel ball on the track represents the degree of closeness in the relationship. The forces that draw a person from the "mere acquaintance" position to "casual friend" are the very same ones that pull a person from "fishing buddy" to "close confidant." The farther up the incline you go, the greater the magnetic pull has to be to overcome the natural forces that pull people apart. I've asked you to select someone toward the higher end so we can examine the force field when it's operating full blast. For me that person is my friend Bill.

Bill and I have known each other for twenty-five years. We first met at seminary where he was two years ahead of me. We were casual friends then but lost touch after he graduated. Seven years later I was on the pulpit committee that called him as pastor of our Presbyterian church. Bill has

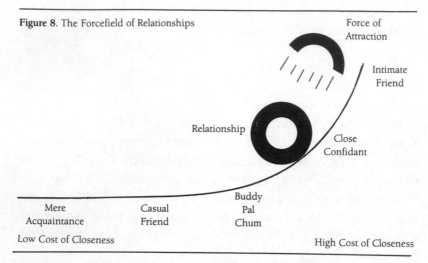

Figure 8. The Forcefield of Relationships

Force of Attraction

Intimate Friend

Relationship

Close Confidant

Buddy
Pal
Chum

Mere
Acquaintance

Casual
Friend

Low Cost of Closeness

High Cost of Closeness

a Ph.D. from Edinburgh, a wicked tennis serve, and equal talents in preaching and administration. His oldest boy is my son's best friend.

What is it that makes Bill attractive to me? If I had to crystallize why I want to draw close to him I'd put it this way: *He makes me feel good* about myself!

This statement is a rather broad umbrella to cover many forces of interpersonal attraction, and it needs further explanation. That's what the rest of the chapter is about. I'll lump these forces into three categories: situation, personality and response—the where, the who and the what of attraction. You'll see that the thread of increased self-esteem is woven into each principle of attraction. I'm drawn toward those who help me like myself. In this I'm not alone. See if it doesn't hold true for you as well.

Situation

What are the odds that two people will click? If Jimmy the Greek was making book on my chances of being attracted to Bill, he'd do well to take note of the circumstances surrounding our interaction. Attraction isn't just a matter of the two people involved. There are at least three situational considerations that make a difference.

1. Proximity. Physical proximity enhances attraction.[1] That fact of life

is reflected in the language of friendship. We say that one person is a *close* friend, while another seems *distant*. That's not just metaphor. It consistently works out in practice. The more opportunity you have to bump into another person, the greater the chance you'll find something you appreciate about him or her. I see this happen in an exercise I use in my Interpersonal Communication class. I randomly divide class members into pairs and assign them to spend all day joined together at the wrist with an eighteen-inch rope. Except for occasional five-minute breaks, each student spends seventeen straight hours in the enforced presence of another. I first gave the class this task with a bit of fear and trembling. What if they ended up not being able to stand the sight of each other? ("Familiarity breeds contempt.") I needn't have worried. Most enjoyed the experience greatly, and many became best friends in the class for the rest of the term. One pair even got married.

The advantages of proximity continue as a relationship develops. The greater the physical distance between two people, the greater the cost in time, energy and money just to get together. The heartiest friendships surmount this obstacle, but many collapse from the sheer effort involved. Bill and I were fortunate. Because we were tossed together at our church, we had thirteen years to build a warm friendship. Even now, when he has a different congregation, we can get together in a couple of hours.

Distance can make a difference in romance too. The problems of long distance love are legion. There's a story—perhaps apocryphal—about the couple in love who lived a thousand miles apart. The fellow wrote to the girl faithfully every day. She ended up marrying the postman. "Out of sight, out of mind" reflects the true picture better than "Absence makes the heart grow fonder." Or as the leprechaun in the play *Finian's Rainbow* said, "When I'm not facing the face I fancy, I fancy the face I face."[2]

It's not just the low cost that makes proximity a force in attraction. We all know someone we wouldn't cross the street to see. But continual contact with another often has a mellowing effect. Professor Higgins expresses this well in *My Fair Lady:* "I've grown accustomed to her face."[3] For years disc jockeys have known the positive effects of mere exposure. Listeners will begin to like a song no matter how rotten it is if it's played enough.

Fortunately, human beings have an advantage over mediocre music. We all have many redeeming, winsome qualities. Prolonged association simply makes it easier for others to appreciate them.[4]

2. *Stress*. Imagine you're a college sophomore enrolled in a beginning psychology course at a large university. When you show up at the experimental laboratory to fulfill a course requirement, you're met by a rather sinister-looking man in a white lab coat who's surrounded by an impressive array of electronic gadgetry. He solemnly introduces himself as Dr. Gregor Zilstein of the Medical School's Department of Neurology. He says you are to be part of an experiment on the effect of electric shock. You'll be given shocks of varying intensity through electrodes strapped to your arm while your pulse rate and blood pressure are monitored. He's quite frank about the procedure. If research like this is to do any good, the shocks have to be strong. He admits they'll be quite painful. But with a tight smile he assures you there will be no permanent tissue damage.

How do you feel? Scared! Then the experimenter—in real life, Stanley Schachter—gives you a brief reprieve. It will take him about ten minutes to set up the equipment. You have a choice. Would you rather wait alone or with someone else who is also a subject in the experiment? If you're like most of the people who were actually subjects in Schachter's experiment, you'll decide to wait with a fellow student. Misery loves company.

Why do we seek companions when we're under stress? Perhaps it's simply that the presence of another warm body is reassuring. Think of the ever-tightening circle of children listening to a ghost story. We may also need others to help define what we're actually feeling. We know we're churning inside, but are those feelings fear, anger, shame or what?

Whatever the reason, people are usually more ready to affiliate with others when they're under stress. In another version of the shock study, students met a relaxed, smiling professor. He told them they would receive an electrical shock, but reassured them it would be quite mild—rather like a tickle. Only one-third of this group decided to wait with others. It wasn't going to be a big deal.[5]

So misery loves company—but not just any company. It doesn't help at all when you're feeling lousy but everything is going great for those around you. College kids in the study chose to sweat out the wait with other students only if they were getting zapped too. In the Old Testament, Job didn't appreciate his "comforters" because they couldn't identify with his agony. Apparently we need to modify the adage to read, "Misery loves miserable company."

We aren't going to have to deal with "Dr. Zilstein," but we can see this principle at work in everyday life: we're attracted to those who share the same stress experience. Many enduring friendships were cemented in London bomb shelters or Vietnam foxholes. The New York power blackout of 1965 and the Chicago snowstorm of 1979 fostered a camaraderie not usually felt in the big city. Spouses of alcoholics seek comfort and understanding in Alanon from people whose lives are similarly disrupted. Guys and girls who have just experienced the emotional pang of breaking up are particularly vulnerable to love on the rebound. Ricochet romance is a classic phenomenon.

Sometimes stress is engineered to promote cohesion. I once knew a youth director who seriously considered hiring someone to throw a rock through the church basement window during a meeting. The kids were fragmented into many cliques, and he knew that a common enemy can foster group solidarity. Football coaches, encounter group trainers and leaders of Outward Bound treks count on the effects of stress to mold a close-knit group.

Over the years Bill and I have shared mutual anxiety over our boys' development. Together we've withstood outside attacks on youth programs for which we were responsible. He's fond of telling the story of a turbulent airplane flight we made together in a snowstorm, which almost ended in a forced landing. Instead of driving us apart, these experiences have cemented our friendship. Common stress draws people together.

3. *Cooperation.* In Rodgers and Hammerstein's musical *Oklahoma* there's a song called "The Farmer and the Cowman." With tongue in cheek, the lyrics say the two men should be friends in spite of their differences: "One man likes to chase a cow; The other likes to push a plow. The cowman ropes a cow with ease; the farmer steals her butter and cheese." They're competing for the same land. They're opponents in the quest for govern-

ment funds. The fences that help the farmer frustrate the cowman. And water is the ultimate wedge that drives them apart—both groups need it to prosper and there's not enough to go around. After listing their separate orientations, the song boldly proclaims: "But that's no reason why they can't be friends."[6] Actually, those are very good reasons!

Competition hinders attraction. It's tough to warm up to people you think are taking the bread off your plate. It's not even necessary that they be the real culprit. Any scapegoat will do when you're frustrated. The classic example is Hitler's tragic success in channeling the frustration of the down-trodden Germans and directing it toward the Jews. We have our own example in U. S. history. When things got tough for the poor Southern farmers, they would lash out at the Negro. One study has documented the extremely high correlation between the price of cotton and the number of lynchings over a period of fifty years. When the price per acre went down, lynchings went up.[7] Christians aren't immune to this tendency. Evangelicals have tended to blame "liberals" for everything from declining morals to sunspots. Mutual appreciation is tough when two people have locked horns. "Worthy adversaries" usually like each other only in fiction.

By contrast, cooperation fosters attraction. This fact was dramatically demonstrated in a field study at a boys' camp. At the start of the summer the guys were divided into two groups, the Bull Dogs and the Red Devils. Through a systematic program of competition and petty pranks they came to view each other as enemies. They hated each other's guts. Then the camp administrators tried various ways to encourage attraction. The counselors sang the praises of the other group, but the kids would have none of it. They brought the kids together at a party. Surely friendly, convivial activity would help. It didn't work. The party turned out to be just another occasion to reinforce already existing prejudice.

Then the staff tried a new approach. They created a series of real-life emergencies such as a broken water pipe that could be solved only by the guys' working together. Slowly the Red Devils began to see signs of humanity in the Bull Dogs. The Bull Dogs began to admit that the Red Devils weren't so bad after all. Working together to achieve a mutual goal fosters attraction.[8]

"I have been saddened to hear that, despite the recent restrictions on your freedom,
many of you still do not like me."

Bill and I have worked together on a number of projects at our church.
We helped start a couples' sharing group. We searched together to find
a youth director. Long-range planning, a "Pass-It-On" evangelism series,
the search for an appropriate missions thrust—all of these formed a coop-

erative backdrop which made Bill easy to like.

What practical advice can you glean from all this? If you want someone to like you, let the situation help. Work to spend lots of time in the person's vicinity. Try to share times of mutual stress and look for opportunities for joint effort. There's no ironclad guarantee that the other person will respond, but your efforts can at least open up the possibility. Whether or not things work out may well depend on what sort of person you are. We'll deal with personality traits next.

Personality

1. *Physical attraction.* You may balk at listing physical attributes under the category of personality just as you might question last chapter's claim that body shape communicates something of who we are. We want to believe we can separate a person's outer looks and inner qualities. Theoretically it's possible, but in practice it's tough. It's especially hard in male-female relationships.

College freshmen at the University of Minnesota were given a chance to sign up for a computer dance. Over seven hundred applied. A panel of upperclassmen secretly rated the students' physical attractiveness as they walked up to the registration table in the student union. Because the raters had only five seconds to score their impressions, they had to make snap judgments free from such considerations as conversational ability, dancing skill, family backgrounds and so on. Unbeknown to the students, there was no computer. The match-ups were made at random. During the intermission at the dance the freshmen were asked how satisfied they were with their blind dates. Satisfaction levels closely paralleled the secret attractiveness ratings. Good-looking partners were a source of pleasure; homely partners were not. The difference showed up in future dating: cute girls were asked for a second date; less attractive girls were not.[9]

I'm bothered by this study. I would like to say this could happen only at a secular college dance, which is more like a meat market than a social activity. But I'm aware that my own Christian college publishes a "Who's New" booklet every fall containing pictures of all the incoming freshmen. Upperclassmen eagerly await its appearance. They circle the photos of girls

Reprinted with permission from the Saturday Evening Post Society, a division of BFL & MS, Inc. © 1986.

"What happened to sis? Best skater on the rink, and suddenly she forgot how!"

they like and make their social plans accordingly. I also realize that, all things being equal, I'd rather be with a good-looking girl than an unattractive one.

Up to this point I've talked about physical attractiveness as if it were a universally recognized commodity, easily measured. Is this the case? For instance, do all upperclassmen circle the same pictures? Not entirely. Let's take a look at some of the variables.

Because I had a beard for fifteen years, I'm intrigued by an experiment that tested people's response to facial hair. Eight fully bearded men in their twenties agreed to be shaved by the same barber. The experimenter took pictures of them in four different stages: full beard, goatee, mustache and clean-shaven.

The young audience that viewed the photographs were most attracted to the bearded faces, less to those with goatees and mustaches, and least to the clean-shaven faces. Men with full beards were considered more masculine, mature, good-looking, dominant, self-confident, courageous, liberal, nonconformist and industrious. The experimenter suggested wryly that in every man there is a beard screaming to be let out.[10] Regardless, it proves that beauty is in the eye of the beholder. To the college-age audience of the survey, my beard would have looked great. In another fellowship it might have aroused disgust. We can talk about standards of attraction only within a given culture.

There seems to be some agreement within our American society about what's desirable. Obesity, for example, is not. There may have been a time when the pleasingly plump shape of a Rubens model was in vogue, but not today. Fat is out, thin is in. That's true in all sorts of transactions, not just romantic relationships. One study found that admissions directors tend to discriminate against overweight college applicants. Consciously or sub-consciously, they associate excess pounds with laziness and lack of will power.[11] Is this fair? Probably not. But just or no, people usually assume that a handsome exterior surrounds a whole bushel basket full of other fine qualities.

I think physical appearance was a factor in my initial friendship with Bill. His athletic 6'6" frame is the envy of many men. He has deep, pene-trating eyes that light up when his face creases in a smile. Even when I knew little about him I automatically assumed that anyone with his rugged good looks and commanding stature must be a good guy.

For those who feel they aren't good-looking, there's an encouraging note: physical attraction has its greatest impact at first impression. After that its importance diminishes rapidly.[12] Lack of physical comeliness puts a per-son at a disadvantage, but not an insurmountable one. As Christians, we need to make a conscious commitment to look for God's beautiful gifts that may be hidden inside some rather plain packages.

2. *Similarity.* I've always been intrigued by the verbal ballet that goes on when two people meet for the first time. Each party drops catchwords to see if the other will latch onto them. Pilots use flying jargon—the back side of the power curve, density altitude and omni navigation. Advocates of Transactional Analysis lace their conversation with phrases about letting the child out, hooking the adult and rewriting the life script. Christians are not immune. Evangelicals sprinkle their discussion with personal references to being born again, being led by the Spirit or getting into the Word.

What's going on? Why this linguistic dance? Perhaps it's an unfair analogy, but I get the impression of two dogs circling and tentatively sniffing each other to determine if they're the right kind. This happens with humans. We're uncomfortable until we have the other guy pegged. We're trying to figure out if we're similar because we like those who are like us.[13]

Probably no principle of interpersonal attraction is so thoroughly researched as "Birds of a feather flock together." Scientists have used the "phantom other" technique to systematically test the effects of similarity on attraction. A person is asked to fill out a lengthy questionnaire about his background, attitudes and personality. Later he's given the chance to read through surveys supposedly filled out by two other people. He's told that he'll have the chance to meet with one of the two, and that he can choose whichever one he likes. In reality there are no other respondents. The experimenter has filled out the two questionnaires based on the subject's own answers. In one case he completes the form so that there's seventy-five per cent agreement with the original responses; in the other, he sets up a twenty-five per cent correspondence. Almost without exception, people choose to meet the more similar person.[14]

There's no question that I quickly identified with Bill. Both of us are competitive on the golf course and tennis court. We share a mutual respect for the power of the spoken word. We're equally harsh in condemning phoniness—game playing in relationships. Both of us are highly task-oriented, each with a drive to achieve. We have matching educational

"We had a hunch they'd be perfect for each other."

degrees and a similar sense of humor. And of course we're committed to the same Lord.

Similarity is a broad term. It can refer to personality, background or attitudes. Which kind has the strongest influence on attraction? Similarity of personality isn't crucial.[15] Sometimes when we see close friends together we're struck by an almost identical trait—the way they laugh, for instance. But this kind of similarity is often the result of friendship, not the cause. It grows out of long hours spent together. In fact, similarity of personality can even work against friendship if the other reveals a trait you don't like in yourself. I have a tendency to duck conflict. I have to make a conscious effort to deal honestly with my own anger. In contrast, Bill is more direct when he's mad. The difference makes me appreciate him even more.

Background is more important than personality. Because we're all prisoners of our past, the way we were brought up limits our chances of appreciating someone from a different subculture. One survey of a thousand men showed overwhelmingly that their best friends shared their same economic, social and religious backgrounds.[16] These family characteristics shape our attitudes.

Without question, attitude similarity is where the real action is. We automatically assume that our friends will agree with us on crucial issues. It always comes as a bit of a shock when they don't. As Hugo Bohun in

Disraeli's *Lothair* said, "My idea of an agreeable person is one who agrees with me."

Isn't all this agreement boring? What ever happened to "Opposites attract?" It just doesn't work that way in most friendships. There are of course some differences of opinion between Bill and me. Bill's view of parachurch organizations is less sympathetic than mine. But this divergence only adds spice to a friendship rooted in common beliefs.

Romance is the one area where opposites appear to attract. Some love theorists (aren't we all) have suggested a complementary-needs hypothesis—that people fall in love with those who fill in the gaps in their lives.[17] Spenders marry savers; introverts marry extroverts. Those aesthetically inclined pick partners with a practical bent. Although there's little solid evidence to back it up, I'm unwilling to dismiss the idea of complementary needs out of hand. The theory seems to make sense, and it happens to reflect Jeanie's and my relationship. I've always pictured the perfect symbiotic couple as a masochist marrying a sadist. But even then there would be similarity. As one psychiatrist has observed, "Two neurotics look for each other with uncanny regularity."[18] But note that these complementary differences are in the area of personality, not attitudes. All agree that common values are crucial in a successful marriage.

Why is similarity such a key element in choosing friends? The answer lies in our overriding need for self-esteem. It's an uncertain world. Most of us have some lingering doubts about our attitudes and lifestyle. Having people close who think and feel as we do can be very comforting. The law of selective exposure suggests that we avoid information that challenges our beliefs.[19] Friendship is probably the purest form of selecting our own propaganda. Relationships with similar others helps us feel OK about who we are.

3. *Competence.* "Everybody loves a winner." Like all truisms, this one is subject to qualification. Jealousy may creep in, or the winner can become insufferable if he gloats about his victory. But in the main, people flock to life's winners and avoid the losers. It reminds me of Groucho Marx's bittersweet comment, "I wouldn't be caught dead joining any club that would have me as a member."

"Bobby . . . Do you like me for myself or for my fast ball?"

A friend's ability may have immediate cash value for us. I know a number of men who have found better jobs through the good offices of a well-placed friend. "It's not what you know but who you know" is a cynical statement of this fact of life. A reflected glory comes from associating with the shakers and movers of this world. Rock star "groupies," sports autograph hounds, political hangers-on, and blind devotees of religious leaders all hope some of the success will rub off on them. There's a more noble reason for being attracted to those who are competent. Down deep we tend to believe that there may be some justice in this world after all. We have the sneaking suspicion that people usually get what they deserve. Thus a person's success becomes prima-facie evidence that he or she deserves our appreciation.[20]

Can a person be too good? In terms of attraction, yes! There comes a point at which another person is so capable that she seems unreal. We want our heroes to be human. Social scientists have discovered that a highly respected leader becomes even more attractive if he or she occasionally stumbles or goofs. They label this the "pratfall effect."[21]

I once counseled a student who had me on a pedestal. This uncomfortable awe strained our relationship. In the midst of one discussion I accidentally spilled a cup of hot chocolate all over my sport coat and tie. I jumped up and went to the men's room to repair the damage, mentally cursing myself for looking like an incompetent fool. I figured that my klutzy behavior had blown any chance to help the guy. Quite the contrary. When I came back the atmosphere was pleasantly different. The student felt free to be more open about his personal problems. As he shyly admitted, "I like you better with cocoa stains on your tie."

Be careful how you apply this discovery. I haven't taken to spilling cups of coffee on purpose. In most cases it would lower my credibility. The pratfall effect increases attraction only when the person seems unapproachable. What's taking place is a certain leveling of status. It's possible to feel genuine affection for another person and yet have things out of kilter regarding power. On the one end of the scale is awe or reverence. That gives away too much. On the other end is paternalistic protection. That assumes too much control. Friendship thrives on a parity of power.

Bill was both competent and approachable, and this made it easy to get close to him. Not only did I feel warm vibrations between us; I also saw in him a man I could respect. I particularly admired his ability to take responsibility for his own life. He seemed to arrive at his attitudes and actions through conscious choice. Never once did I get the impression he was trapped or helpless. His confident exercise of freedom was attractive.

Response

We now come to the most important part of attraction. I don't want to discount the ones we've already discussed. The situational factors increase our readiness for intimacy and the personality factors narrow the field of those who are eligible. But taken alone, these factors don't draw us into a close friendship. For that we require a response. We need some sign that the other person feels the way we do. Closeness comes only through reciprocity—mutual attraction.[22] Its presence can leapfrog us into intimacy. Its absence puts a damper on any relationship.

In 200 B.C. the Roman Necato advised that he would reveal a love potion without drug or herb or any other spell. His advice: If you wish to be loved, love. We're less eloquent today, but the advice is the same: "If you want a friend, be a friend." The final three factors—affirmation, favors and touch—are ways of showing people you care for them.

1. *Affirmation.* Forty years ago Dale Carnegie wrote *How To Win Friends and Influence People,* which has sold over a million copies. (As an author, I'm envious.) Carnegie claimed that everyone has a "gnawing and unfaltering human hunger" for appreciation.[23] His advice was simple: if you want somebody to like you, heap on the praise.

Carnegie's blunt suggestion brought a storm of protest. Critics snidely referred to his book as *The Art of Groveling.* But his basic idea has been upheld not only in bookstore sales, but also in the research laboratory. We *do* have a tremendous appetite for social approval, and we tend to like those who feed us goodies. Call it what you will—affirmation, praise, verbal stroking, flattery, giving warm fuzzies, building up another—we appreciate those who appreciate us.

Can't praise be inappropriate or overdone? Yes, sometimes enough is enough. I'll note some qualifications in the next few paragraphs. But I want to stress here that these exceptions do not invalidate the general rule. More than any other factor, affirmation comes the closest to being the "irresistible force" of attraction.

Ingratiation is one exception. Even faint praise is too much if we feel the other guy is trying to get something in return. There's no exact rule of thumb to tell us when this is happening. It's tough enough to spot our own motivations, much less figure out the whys and wherefores of someone else's action. But we discount compliments if we conclude the other fellow is angling for a favor.[24] We want our praise with no strings attached.

One hot issue in attraction research centers around the appreciation vs. accuracy struggle. Would we rather get an honest evaluation of what we do than hear unmitigated praise? The answer is a definite and positive maybe. If our work is important to us and we know it's not quite right, we appreciate the person who gives constructive criticism. Conversely, we lose respect for the critic who compliments a slipshod performance. But if we're uncertain about the quality of our work, or if the evaluation reflects upon us personally, we'd rather hear only raves. We don't look kindly on the bold friend who tells us we have bad breath. We may mumble our thanks and switch brands of toothpaste, but the relationship suffers.[25]

Praise is like the dollar. Its value fluctuates according to supply and demand. A few years back a man I knew slightly came up to me after church. "I just want to tell you, Em, how impressed I am with you. You're the greatest guy in the world." Wow! How's that for affirmation? I felt a warm rush of appreciation for this noble soul I'd previously overlooked. While I was basking in the glow of his compliment, he called over another member of the congregation. Clapping his arm around the fellow's shoulder, he said, "Em, you know Bob, don't you? He's the greatest guy in the world." It was probably childish on my part, but the fact that there were now two of us at the summit took some of the steam out of the original comment. Praise means more when it's selective.[26]

It also means more when it's unexpected. Suppose you've been at odds with someone. She's always been slightly aloof. Then out of the blue you notice a warmth creeping into her comments. You pick up an implied compliment. Finally you hear a flat-out statement of appreciation. You'll probably feel more grateful to this convert than you will toward another who has always been in your fold. It's easy to take someone for granted if she's unfailingly positive.[27]

This has implications for how we handle conflict. If we are always papering over our anger in the cause of harmony, our continuous string of positive remarks may fall on deaf ears. I'm not suggesting we stir up wrath. But if we deal with our natural irritations in an open way, our subsequent comments of appreciation will have fresh impact.

Bill can get mad. A few times in the course of our relationship he has been justifiably peeved at me. His eyes flash and his voice carries an edge as he expresses his anger. Quite frankly, I don't like it. But those times of irritation make subsequent words of appreciation even nicer. "Em, we've been through a lot together. You're my good friend. I'm glad." Me too.

That affirmation would turn to ashes if I felt it was insincere or angling for special favors. But I don't. Bill's words have greater impact because they are salted with moments of honest doubt and constructive criticism. And the few times he's pulled back in the relationship have merely served to make the subsequent warm words more welcome.

2. *Favors.* Favors are compliments with legs. Bill has shown appreciation with actions as well as words. Our history includes guest rounds of golf, leisurely barbecued meals, shared vacations and the gift of a listening ear when things are rough. Strange as it may seem, one of Bill's most valued gifts to me was a fresh trout. Bill and his wife came to a surprise fortieth birthday party. The fish was to commemorate my ongoing love affair with Trout Island in the middle of Lake Michigan. It was special that they made the effort to tailor-make the gift to the man. The fish and the friendship both tasted good.

All of the qualifications I listed for affirmation apply equally to favors. We don't appreciate a favor if we feel obligated to do something in return or if the gift is inappropriately large. The unexpected favor has more impact than one that's as predictable as clockwork.

There's a surprising twist to this business of doing favors—although we're drawn toward those who do nice things for us, we're even more attracted to those who let us do nice things for them.[28] I discovered this when I worked with high-school kids in Young Life. I used to do all sorts of things to try to build closeness with non-Christians. I drove kids to football games, conducted a free pilots' ground school, stuffed colored napkins in a homecoming float. Then one day I needed a ride to the airport. Jeanie was busy, and I couldn't get an airport limousine on short notice. In desperation I called one of the Young Life fellows who had a car and asked him for a lift. He was happy to oblige. He wouldn't even let me pay for the gas. We drew closer as a result of this forty-five-minute trip than we had in the whole previous year.

After this I made it a practice to ask different kids for a ride to the plane whenever I went out of town. I also looked for other ways to let them show they cared. I even had a guy come over to help me bathe our basset hound. As long as there was a base level of attraction to begin with, calling on another for an occasional favor somehow strengthened the bond between us. This doesn't mean I quit trying to serve them. I just let them get in on part of the action as well.

3. *Touch.* Touch is an intensifier. Whatever we feel about another per-

son, we'll feel it more so after physical contact. If I'm turned off by another in the first place, the intrusion of his hand against me is an unwelcome violation of my privacy. I recall an overfamiliar Texan who was trying to sell me insurance. "You know, pardner, I want what's best for you," he drawled—punctuating his words with a hearty slap on the back. Mild irritation turned into full-blown revulsion. If you want to use touch as a way of forging a relationship, be doubly careful to check out whether the other party is up for it. The results can be spectacular if you miscalculate.

If I already like a person, touch can tap into a whole reservoir of warm feelings. Appreciation can deepen into long-term emotional attachment. Avoiding touch in such circumstances would create an artificial barrier. When Jeanie was in the hospital for major surgery, Bill spent the entire morning in the waiting room sweating it out with me. Two different times he wrapped his big arms around me in a bearlike embrace. No other means could have so adequately demonstrated our solidarity. It would have been a travesty of friendship if he had merely reached out and shaken hands.

I place a high value on touch in a relationship. Perhaps this is because I have a touch-oriented family. It's still natural for Jeanie and me to hug our adult son and daughter. For years the four of us would sit squeezed together on the sofa watching TV. When our basset hound was alive, we loved to see if eight massaging hands could make him collapse into a contented heap. I believe there's a place for the physical expression of intimacy outside the home as well. I realize this is a "touchy" issue for some Christians, but I think there's a standard of touch behavior that facilitates healthy relationships and is pleasing to God.

Touch is out of bounds when it's used to create or experience a closeness that's not there, but it is appropriate when it reflects an intimacy that already exists. This standard suggests that touching, like any other human behavior, is a matter of conscious choice. I'm not an animal that must react to every urge within. I can be selective. The principle also means that I won't employ touch as a means to instant intimacy. There's no question that touch can be used as a method of leapfrogging into emotional closeness, but to do so is to misuse its potential. Friendship is a process. If physical closeness short-circuits the natural growth of a relationship, I'll end up feeling a strong attraction that lacks substance. I've always been leery of the sloppy-agape type of person who goes around indiscriminately hugging others he barely knows.

Touch is a natural and enjoyable expression of affection. From the day we're born we reach out to hold what we like. This physical contact is healthy when it's based on mutual emotional ties that have already developed. In these cases touch not only reflects an ongoing friendship, it's an added impetus to future attraction.

At the outset of this chapter I said we're attracted to those who make us feel good about ourselves. By now you've probably picked up the idea that my relationship with Bill does just that. How about the friend you've had in mind the past few minutes? My guess is that he or she fits the profile I've sketched in figure 9.

Figure 9. What Attracts Us to Each Other

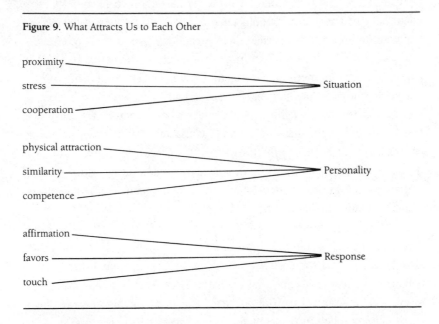

Exceptions are possible. The circumstances surrounding our meeting may be so fraught with anxiety that I simply retreat into my shell. The other person may be so good-looking that I feel inferior. Unwanted favors may

leave me feeling uncomfortably obligated. But friendship is not accidental. If all the factors I've listed are present, attraction is an almost foregone conclusion. Even when a few of them are missing, a strong magnetic pull is likely.

We aren't slaves to these forces. The very awareness of their existence can equip us to override our natural tendencies. This is especially true if we meet someone lacking the compelling features I've discussed. Scripture is clear that God has a special identification with those on the margin of society—the hungry, the poor, the prisoners, the oppressed. In the world's eyes these folks are usually among the unlovely. Commitment to Christ can motivate us to draw close to those whom we might otherwise ignore.

Drawing close is what the final three chapters are about. Two people can feel an irresistible attraction toward each other, but that's no guarantee they'll end up friends. Attraction is a no-effort response. Friendship is another matter. The process of developing intimacy involves risk. We might get burned. By advocating interpersonal closeness, I may be setting you up for a fall. But I'm convinced that friendship is vital, and that we should enter into it with our eyes wide open. Understanding the dynamics of intimate relationships can lower the risks.

UNDERSTANDING WE

8

TRUST
AND
TRANSPARENCY

*To reveal oneself openly and honestly
takes the rawest kind of courage.*

I WAS TALKING ABOUT MY family when I was a kid. We were halfway on the drive from Champaign to Wheaton—one hundred fifty miles of flat farmland in the winter, the kind of journey that loosens the tongue. A former Wheaton College student who had transferred to the University of Illinois was going back for a reunion. I'd been in Champaign to consult with a fellow communications professor. It wasn't by chance that the two of us rode north together. We had a growing appreciation of each other that blurred teacher/student lines. Now I spoke of those early years.

I talked about my shy but talented father who died too young—an alcoholic. Then I described my gregarious mother who was felled by an incurable cancer, and my depressed sister who took her own life with a gun rather than face a joyless future. When I added that my older brother died of pneumonia before I was born, I was overwhelmed by a feeling of aloneness. Tears flooded my eyes, and I had to pull onto the shoulder of the interstate lest I lose control of the car and join the other Griffins.

Once the car was stopped I lost control. I sobbed over the steering wheel in the realization that none of my people were behind me to act as a backstop; I had no family member to turn to for advice, no parents to offer praise or encouragement. Sensitive beyond years, my young friend let me feel my grief without interruption, offering only an outreached hand of support.

I had a eureka experience out there on Interstate 57. I write of it for three reasons. First, it was pivotal in my understanding of the place of friends in my life. For the past decade I've worked hard at my friendships. Now I realize why. Friends are my family. It's not surprising that I see this chapter on drawing close to others as the most important one in the book.

Second, I mention that experience to introduce the idea of trust. Trust is the precondition for true intimacy—the oxygen that makes the fire blaze. To see why trust is so crucial, picture me as a large round Spanish onion driving on I-57. I'm not suggesting that you think of me as having Latin ancestry, bad breath or the ability to make my passenger cry. Rather I want you to imagine me with concentric layers of personhood. There's Em Griffin's outer skin that's open for all the world to see—professor, father, driver of a Dodge Aries. These characterizations are really me, but there's much more dwelling beneath the surface. My friend could have taken a knife, cut through the outer layers, and discovered an inner man not available to everyone—a teacher inordinately excited when a student likes his course, a dad that isn't at all sure he has expected enough from his kids, a driver that doesn't give a rip for the car he's driving but has a passion for airplanes. As a matter of fact, in our brief friendship we'd already reached that intermediate level. There was an even deeper inner core, however, that so far had been too tough to penetrate. The layers were tightly wrapped, offering great resistance to any blade trying to cut to the center.

The onion/knife analogy isn't original with me. It's the picture suggested in Social Penetration Theory as a model of how people become close friends.[1] The image of a probing knife strikes some as too clinical to represent what they see as a warm fuzzy process. But I think it is an apt description of the risk that goes with friendship. One can get hurt.

Would my rider want to hear about the inner Em Griffin? To penetrate deeply into someone else's life requires concerted effort in the present with an implied commitment for the future. In this age of "keeping our options open," that could be too great a responsibility for many people.

Would I in turn want to be known? To allow someone in that deep is to risk embarrassment or rejection. The safe course is to remain a private person. It takes an atmosphere of mutual trust to overcome the risk of vulnerability. That's why the first half of this chapter deals with trust.

The third reason for recounting my drive through the past is to introduce the idea of transparency. It's one thing to be attracted to another person. It's quite another to draw close and develop an in-depth relationship. The former is simple fascination; the latter is friendship. The one is interest; the other is intimacy. Trust is the climate for transparency, but no closeness takes place until the knife moves inward. Social Penetration theory labels the inward thrust of the blade into a willing onion _self-disclosure_. It's the process through which people get close—the stuff of friendship. The bond between two people was irrevocably altered that day on the interstate. Because self-disclosure is the high-protein food of relationships, the second half of this chapter will examine the best way to slice the onion.

Friendship under the Microscope

Once I realized that, for me, friendship was not a luxury, I threw myself into exploring the dynamics of closeness. My appointment book, letter file and phone bill of the last few years are records of that quest. "Friends are those we waste time on"—and I can't think of a more enjoyable way of blowing major hunks of each month. But I also decided to investigate close relationships through systematic research at my college. The result was an extensive study of intimacy using sixty pairs of best friends.[2]

I recruited college students by announcements in classes, notices in the campus newspaper and posters in the student union. I offered the enticement of free pizza or dinner for two at McDonald's, but the real draw for students seemed to be the fun of exploring their relationship. To be included in the study, each member of a pair had to state privately that the other was his or her best friend on campus—that no closer friends were around.

Since I used no absolute standard of relational depth, I expected to find a wide range of intimacy among these friends. I was particularly keen on discovering differences in four separate types of friendships: guy-guy, girl-girl, guy-girl (romantic) and guy-girl (platonic). Therefore I recruited fifteen pairs of each type. I used a number of measures of interpersonal closeness to determine the nature of the relationships:

☐ An exercise like TV's *Newlywed Game* to determine past level of self-disclosure.

☐ Ten rounds of Password to assess communication efficiency.

☐ A self-reported touch survey describing the level of tactile intimacy.

☐ A "protection of partner" checklist indicating what topics are too painful to discuss with the friend.

☐ A 0 to 100% scale on which to rank commitment to remain close friends after graduation.

☐ A 0 to 100% scale on which to measure certainty that they'd live in geographical proximity to each other after graduation.

☐ A perceived status form on which to rank the friend as higher or lower than themselves in physical attractiveness, spiritual maturity, intelligence, social skills, athletic ability and financial position.

As I expected, there were tremendous differences among pairs on these seven measures of closeness. Surprisingly, however, the discrepancies were not among the four friendship types. For example, the males evidenced as much depth in their relationships as the females did. The main overall difference between the pairs was their inner attitude of trust. I hadn't expected to find this, but the closer the relationship, the higher the two friends scored on a simple sixteen-item true/false survey measuring level of trust.[3] Take a look at some of the items on this survey. Every one reflects confidence in the other person—who that person is and what he or she might do.

☐ I respect his/her individuality.

☐ I like him/her just as he/she is with no change.

☐ I want what is best for him/her.

☐ I feel I can say anything to him/her.

☐ My relationship with him/her is characterized by trust.

Folks answering true to these statements showed high levels of intimate communication—self-disclosure, touch, "Password" efficiency and non-defensive feedback. They also indicated they had a high commitment to future friendship. In other words, trust is the source of a whole batch of relational goodies.

The Teflon of Trust

It's hard to tell whether an action springs from trust or from some other

"Of course I trust you. I just feel a little uneasy about letting you have the keys."

attitude. Suppose, for example, I hand you the keys to my new car. Outside observers might conclude that I trust you—and they'd probably be right. But a number of other possibilities come to mind. Maybe I've hurt you deeply and this is my way of trying to make things right. Perhaps I'm filthy rich or have an insurance company that is, so the risk strikes me as minimal. It's possible that I feel tremendous social pressure from our mutual friends to go against my better judgment. Perhaps I'm so dumb I don't realize your two previous accidents and seven moving violations have anything to say about future performance. Or maybe I'm just a martyr at heart.

My point is that behavior alone can fake us out. Trust is an internal attitude. We can see that in this definition: "Trust is a general expectation that the promises of other individuals with regard to the future can be relied on."[4]

The closest friendship pairs in my study seemed to expect the best from each other. How come?

For some, the world is a benign place. Doors needn't be locked; a man's word is his bond; buses run on time. We're quick to label Charlie Brown's irrepressible optimism naive. But it's a naiveté that's encouraged in Scripture. "Love believes all things, hopes all things" (1 Cor 13:7 RSV). This time Lucy will hold the ball.

Others take a dim view of the human condition. They suspect that, left to their natural devices, people will lie, rape, pillage and loot. They observe the human race and declare everyone a loser. But all is not bleak, because their suspicions are countered by their confidence in God's intervention. They know that "in all things God works for the good" (Rom 8:28). They count on others to act in a beneficial way because of God's guiding hand.

Still others trust themselves. They figure that people are like almost everything else—some are good and some are bad. Taking seriously the biblical admonition to "test the spirits" (1 Jn 4:1), they have confidence in their ability to winnow out those who will deal with them fairly. They're willing to bet that selection of a trustworthy friend is an art they've mastered well.

Finally, there are those who trust because trust produces positive results.

Trust others and they'll be trustworthy. Doubt them and your doubts will be confirmed. These people see trust as a self-fulfilling prophecy. The mere expectation of the event makes it come true. In that sense, these high trusters are convinced that the locus of control is within themselves.

Regardless of why it's there, trust does nice things for a relationship. Most folks enjoy being around high-trusting individuals. (How strange!) The suspicious Eeyores are not nearly so much fun. Not only is the trusting person better liked; he or she usually becomes the recipient of others' trust. It's like a breeder reactor: trust begets trust.

But isn't all this trusting setting folks up for a fall? Don't "Boy Scouts" and do-gooders get burned more often than those with street smarts?

Apparently not. The suspicions of those who view others through jaundiced eyes seem to set off warning alarms. Not wanting to get hurt, others launch pre-emptive strikes.[5] Thus the nontrusting person fosters the defensive approach of "do unto others before they do unto you." Of course, the results merely confirm the nontrusters' suspicions. You can't convince them that their own doubting attitude increases the odds of a surprise attack. But it does.

What if I have trouble trusting others? Am I doomed for life to be suspicious of every motive, to doubt all expressions of feeling, to be wary of each person's willingness to deliver on promises? Fortunately, no. Just as muscles can be developed, so can interpersonal trust. The key in both cases is exercise.

I'm on somewhat shaky ground here, because I'm a stranger to Nautilus equipment and barbells. But my friends who are shaped like inverted triangles assure me that low-weight repetition, not pumping huge amounts of iron a few times, is the way to build strength. So it is with trust.

Some people are impressed by heroic acts of blind faith that put you at maximum risk. Rappelling off a cliff while another holds the rope, confessing hidden sin to a new acquaintance, allowing someone else to invest your life's savings—these look like acts of maximum trust. In fact, they may be mere foolhardiness. Even if you don't get stung, you have done nothing to make trust easier the next time.

Consider, however, the following everyday choices:

☐ Hearing an ambiguous message and assuming the best until you can check it out.

☐ Believing what another says, even if it sounds improbable.

☐ Accepting a bill from a plumber, auto mechanic or dentist as reasonable.

☐ Viewing another's conception of God's will as equally valid as yours.

☐ Assuming that the other party can handle an expression of a deeply felt emotion.

As trust goes, these are lightweight exercises. But when a slight risk is taken over and over without mishap, a deep-seated attitude of trust is formed. Practice makes permanent.

Let's now go back to the onion. The way to get close to people is to become transparent, to let them penetrate to my inner core. I wouldn't let them try unless I felt a powerful attraction. But a magnetic pull alone isn't enough to form a close relationship. My inner layers are so tightly wrapped that the blade can't overcome the resistance unless it's coated with a nonstick layer of Teflon. Trust is the Teflon of intimacy.

Transparency

"Now we see through a glass, darkly," says Paul in 1 Corinthians 13:12 (KJV), "but then face to face: now I know in part; but then shall I know even as also I am known." He's writing, of course, about our relationship with God. But this ideal image of mutual transparency is also the standard of closeness on the human level. For most folks, having intimate talks with another is the operational definition of friendship.[6] This is true not only in an American context but for other cultures as well. An Arabian proverb holds that a friend is "one to whom one may pour out all the contents of one's heart, chaff and grain together, knowing that the gentlest of hands will take and sift it, keep what is worth keeping and with the breath of kindness blow the rest away."

The proverb not only underscores the centrality of self-disclosure in friendship; it also recognizes that the listener's response is crucial. Some people, starved for intimacy, try to force others out of their shells. But if you crack an egg with a hammer to hasten the hatching, you usually get a bruised chicken. It's much more effective to create a warm, trusting environment which will incubate friendship.[7] As I've already said, the essence of trust is expecting others to keep their promises. There are at least two implied promises in the act of listening to someone else pour out her heart: first, anything you say will *not* be used against you; and second, I won't blab this around to others. Lucy failed on both counts.

Charlie Brown needs a guideline to minimize the "Lucy liability." We do too. Does such a principle exist? I think so. Five years ago I wrote that reciprocity is the basis for intelligent self-disclosure. Nothing has happened in the intervening time to change my mind; if anything, I'm more committed to dual transparency than before. I've struggled to restate the same truth in new words but find I like best the way I first said it in *Getting Together*.[8]

I have a poster on my office wall that pictures a stylishly drawn turtle with an elongated neck. The caption reads: "Behold the turtle who makes progress only when he sticks his neck out." Many advocates of self-disclosure use the turtle as an example of what *not* to be—retreating into your shell because you're afraid to expose yourself to others. But I see this funny-looking creature as a model of what appropriate disclosure should be. I picture two turtles, face to face, except their heads are almost completely hidden from view. One turtle extends his neck just a bit. It would be foolish to stick it out all the way—he might get his head lopped off. If the other turtle responds in kind then the first one ventures out some more. In a series of minute movements the turtle ends up with his head in the sunshine, but only if his counterpart follows his lead. At any time he's prepared to slow the progression, come to a complete stop or even back off.

There are a number of salient features in my turtle picture. First and foremost is reciprocity. At best, self-disclosure is not a solo act. There is a quid pro quo. "You tell me your dream; I'll tell you mine." The healthiest form of self-presentation is probably that which is just slightly ahead of the norm. . . .

I've tried to capture this idea in the image of my turtle. He takes the initial risk. He's always a tad ahead of the game— testing, probing, hoping. That kind of risk is tied into self-esteem. A person with a low self-image will be scared of the potential scorn from others, and therefore remain silent. But people who have a modicum of self-confidence won't feel like their whole existence hangs in the balance, so they can afford to chance it. At the same time they are constantly monitoring others' responses and are ready to pull back when confronted with indifference or hostility.

Reciprocity is crucial as an indication of the other's internal state of mind. It signals that he's not offended by our initial revelation. Even more important, it shows a willingness to be vulnerable. There's a parity of risk. I've got the goods on him just as much as he does on me. There's a good probability he'll be trustworthy. Finally it reveals a readiness to proceed to deeper levels of intimacy.

The turtle model also focuses on the gradual nature of appropriate self-disclosure. It takes time. Fortunately, proponents of "instant intimacy" are on the decline. I'm not a wine drinker, but the idea of an old vintage

"Just because I'm your pet, you don't own me."

patiently aged in wooden casks holds a certain appeal. Stress conditions can accelerate the friendship process, but the normal pattern is one of slow growth.

It may come as a surprise to readers of my other books, but there's a new feline addition to our household. As Siamese cats go, Mindanao is remarkably nonaloof. She sleeps on my chest at night, bounds after me if I jog through the woods, and curls up on my lap and purrs while I'm reading a book or watching TV. But she likes to pick her times. I typically make the first move toward closeness—calling her, encouraging her to jump into my arms, stroking her fur. Usually I'm rewarded by the sound of her internal motor. But at other times she chooses to keep to herself. If I push it, I'm liable to feel the gentle but firm pressure of her teeth letting me know that now is not the time for closeness.

Intimacy is like that. It's an intricate blend of self-disclosure and independence.[9] If we desire closeness, it's sensible to make the first move. We can open up to the other, sharing a portion of who we are. If the other reciprocates, we can safely reveal more. But we never imagine that our initial openness puts the other under an obligation to respond in kind. We want to get close, but we respect the other person's freedom of choice.

Unfortunately some folks feel their honesty gives them license to demand transparency from others. It doesn't, yet they always seem surprised when their kitten bounds away. That shows a lack of social sensitivity.

Others subscribe to what Keith Miller calls the "vomit theory" of self-disclosure.[10] Instead of revealing their innards gradually they spill their guts to another in one mighty upheaval. This is usually too much to ask a friend to endure.

There's an underlying issue whenever people choose to reveal their inner selves to another—control. Interpersonal intimacy is possible only when there's a parity of power.[11] When I become transparent to someone else, I become vulnerable. Transparency is a giant step toward closeness as long as we're on the same footing. But if you've got the goods on me while remaining inaccessible yourself, the power gap will prevent us from drawing close. You probably would never hurt me. But the potential for one-way harm will always keep me a bit on edge. Intimacy requires _mutual_ control.

To go back to the original onion image, two people draw close only when their spheres of self are penetrated by the other to approximately the same depth. If I've plunged to your inner core, yet you've only pricked my surface, intimacy is still in the future. The knife-into-the-onion analogy suggests one other crucial requirement of transparency for closeness. Up to this point, I've written only of the depth of knowledge. The number of blades penetrating is equally vital.

Many Christians are quick to trade testimonies of how they came to know the Lord. This depth of sharing reflects the trust they have not only in God, but also in each other. The blade has sunk deep, but if that's the only point of contact, the relationship has merely the illusion of intimacy. Closeness comes through multiple penetrations—disclosure in many areas. Let's take a look at four that lay the groundwork for closeness.

"Of course this is confidential. Why did you ask?"

Story

I was recently asked to lead a retreat for a Christian organization to promote closeness among top management. These folks loved the Lord and cared deeply for the people they served, but they were virtual strangers to each other. We spent the entire first day recounting events from our past. People left that day with vivid images of a father saving a dog before it went over a waterfall, a wife faced with a life-support decision for her comatose husband, an Air Force photographer facing death when a "playful" paratrooper tried to pull him along, a supposedly sleeping boy who first realized his father's love from a midnight kiss. These hard-driving executives saw each other through new glasses once they had snapshots from the past. No longer were the others simply cogs in a machine. They became warm beings who had been hurt, held and healed.

Emotions

Feelings are the common currency of humanity. So many other factors drive us apart. We spend a great deal of energy amassing titles, achievements and awards, yet in the end they often isolate rather than unite. I'm proud and pleased that I'm Dr. Griffin, Professor of Communications, Teacher of the Year at Wheaton College, author of a book that received *Group* magazine's Book of the Year Award. But none of this has brought me closer to a single person, and if I'm not careful it may create a barrier. Differences in attitude separate. Diverse backgrounds make it hard to relate. But emotions are the common coin of the realm.

We all hurt, we all laugh, we all fear. To the extent that we share things that make our hearts pound, stomachs tighten and spines tingle, a common bond will draw us together. As I write this, the Chicago Bears have unified my city in a way I haven't seen since I was a kid. Even normally closed men are voicing their excitement and fear as the team faces its first Super Bowl. It's sad that it takes a "super" event to stimulate what should be a normal happening. But whatever the cause, the expression of raw feeling makes for real friendship.

Weakness

Most of us act as if we'd invented sin. We assume others would be horrified if they saw the soft underbelly of our lives, so we show them only the hard shell on top. That's why one theologian claimed there's more fellowship in the average bar than in the Christian church. A lack of fellowship certainly plays havoc in our relationship with God. We can sing "Jesus Loves Me" till we're blue in the face, but unless we experience loving forgiveness from our friends, the words ring hollow. And people can't pardon our actions if they're hidden from view.

James says, "You should get into the habit of admitting your sins to each other" (Jas 5:16 Phillips). He ties this advice in with physical health, perhaps because there's a lot of emotional strain involved in keeping our misdeeds secret. It's like holding a beach ball underwater. It takes constant energy, and the ball is always liable to pop to the surface unexpectedly. James doesn't link confession with interpersonal closeness—but he could.

Despite our fears, most folks are drawn to those who share their human-ness.

Symmetrical pink Christmas trees made of aluminum are machine per-fect, but they're not very approachable. It's true that the cut spruce variety has a bad side: it drops needles on the floor and oozes pitch that sticks to your hands. But it sends out a genuine aroma and a warmth that the artificial tree can't touch. So it is with people. Vulnerability is more win-some than apparent perfection.

Affection

In *The Friendship Factor,* Alan Loy McGinnis flatly states that we should dare to talk about our affection.[12] If we do, we will become irresistible to some. Yet for many, voicing their affinity for another comes harder than admit-ting sin. That's sad. I think of the delightful movie *E.T.* The extraterrestrial visitor lies dormant in a cold coffin, apparently dead. His friend Elliot weeps over his body and sobs, "E.T., I love you." At that point, E.T.'s heartlight glows and the lovable creature revives. But why do we have to wait until someone's dead before we reveal our love?

I once received a note through campus mail from a student with whom I'd had extensive discussions in my office. It came on a card showing a picture from the Metropolitan Museum. It read in part: "This is a print of one of my favorite paintings by Monet. I want to share it with you. Com-pared to the original, it's only a pale reproduction. The original is breath-taking. You, Em, are an original."

Do you think I'd fall for that? You'd better believe it! Mark Twain said, "I can live two months on one good compliment." A sincere expression of affection may last a lifetime.

In addition to the four essential areas of intimacy, there are many other aspects of our lives that we can share. These include how we handle money and how we feel about our bodies, our political attitudes and our food preferences, our personality quirks and so on.[13] No one person can ever know the full spectrum of my life. The more I share with another, the higher the odds that we'll be close. But the four primary areas—story, emotions, weakness and affection—are the most crucial.

When I explored these four areas in the friendship study mentioned earlier in the chapter, I found no differences between male friends and female friends, romantic couples and platonic pairs. That was a bit of a surprise. Common wisdom has it that guys are less open than girls. Yet we have to remember that these were all best friends. It's probably true that guys in casual relationships tend to be more guarded. But transparency is necessary for intimacy. If you're going to be close, you can't be closed.

Of course some folks had disclosed themselves in more areas than others. Width of disclosure—the proportion of life that was an open book to the friend—followed the law of reciprocity. Students who had shared across wide ranges of their lives also knew a great deal about their friends.

I discovered one other fascinating relationship in my systematic study of close friends. There was an overall positive connection between self-disclosure and extent of touch: the more deeply the friends shared their lives with each other, the more likely they were to touch each other. It makes sense—both self-disclosure and touch make a person vulnerable.[14] The one exception to this finding was from romantic couples, whose extent of touching did not increase with their self-disclosure. In fact, they worked against each other. Those high in self-disclosure reported low levels of touch. Those who were physically intimate knew less about their partner's life. The average couple I studied had been dating for twenty-one months, time enough to explore all forms of closeness. Perhaps these couples had reached a decision early as to whether to talk or touch.

Stages of Intimacy

Instant intimacy is a myth. Closeness is a process that's not always quick, smooth or ever increasing. One writer in the field spots ten distinct steps in the life cycle of an intimate relationship.[15] The first five are stages of heightened involvement. The last five are waypoints toward ultimate disengagement. (See figure 10.) Think of a person who's important to you, and see if this list helps you identify where you are in the relationship.

1. _Initiating_—You see some things you like. You're pleasant and upbeat as you open the channels of communication. No knives have yet penetrated the onion's skin, but you're prepared.

Figure 10. Ten Stages of an Intimate Relationship

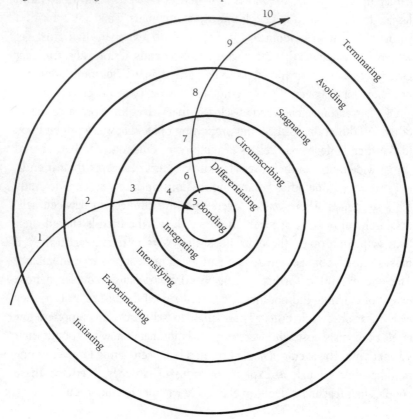

2. *Experimenting*—You attempt to reduce uncertainty. You begin to advertise who you are while seeking to discover similar information about the other. Penetration has begun.

3. *Intensifying*—You disclose yourself in depth to the other person who reciprocates. Most of this chapter applies to the intensifying phase. You begin to refer to the two of you as "we," and you struggle to blend together while holding onto your unique identity.

4. *Integrating*—Coupling becomes a fact. You're fused to the other, because you define who you are in relationship to him or her. Using the onion analogy, many knives have penetrated up to the hilt.

5. *Bonding*—You make a public declaration of closeness. Marriage is the obvious example, but partnership, coauthorship and announced friendship also qualify.

6. *Differentiating*—"Our" becomes "my." You experience periodic conflict and back off on any pressure to penetrate further. The term "parallel partners" is an appropriate label. It's as if the movie projector has stopped and may run backward.

7. *Circumscribing*—You protect your inner layers by avoiding touchy topics. The film is now in slow-motion reverse; the blade is being withdrawn from the onion.

8. *Stagnating*—There is nothing to talk about. You're careful not to offend. The relationship is in full retreat.

9. *Avoiding*—You feel negative vibes in each other's presence. You seek to avoid contact. "I can't stay long" is the theme song as the blade rests uneasily on the onion's surface.

10. *Terminating*—You part ways. Sometimes it's an official divorce, breakup or legal dissolution. More often it's merely a final drifting apart.

Figure 10 on page 182 summarizes these ten stages in light of the onion model we've used throughout. Most relationships never get past the experimenting level, so phases 3 to 7 don't apply. The acquaintance goes from initiating (1) to experimenting (2) and then directly to stagnating (8), avoiding (9) and terminating (10).

Very few relationships move from phase 1 through phase 5 (bonding). Even fewer stay there. It's as if the natural laws of entropy apply not only to thermodynamics but to warmth in friendship as well. Statistically speaking, most relationships terminate before death rather than because of it. That's the bad news.

The good news is that the triumvirate of *attraction, trust* and *transparency* can buck the trend. We don't just drift into closeness. Much less do we stay there without conscious energy and considerable risk. But if vulnerability doesn't scare us off, we just might beat the odds. In order to do so we're going to have to become experts in the twin arts of accountability and forgiveness. They are the next steps in "Understanding We."

9

ACCOUNTABILITY AND FORGIVENESS

Communication is irreversible and unrepeatable.

BRUCE WAS A STRONG, diamond-in-the rough type of guy. His square-cut jaw, inverted triangle physique and tree-trunk thighs gave the impression of a man's man. Yet contrasting with his appearance, his words to me as we walked along the beach were unsure.

"I'm confused, Em. I've heard you speak on youth evangelism twice. You suggest a relational approach that's different from the hard-hitting gospel methods I use. I'm kinda hooked by what you say. That's why I signed up for this off-campus course. I want to watch you in action. I know you once had it with teen-age kids. I think that's because you're loving. But I wonder. . . . Are you really tender with people, or have you just gone soft?"

Good question. I couldn't give him a definitive answer. I simply invited him to take a close look and draw his own conclusions, not at all sure which way his judgment would cut. The issue he raised is a tough one to resolve. Bruce was attracted to the care for others he thought he saw, yet he didn't want to get sucked into wishy-washy relationships devoid of standards of right and wrong. Law and grace—there will always be a tension.

Rollo May views it as an internal balancing act between will and love.[1] Will without love is cruel legalism. You do all the right things, but people get hurt. Love without will is a hippy type of sentiment that has no meaning. "I am not honored by being loved simply because I belong to the genus 'man,' " says May. Relational health thrives only when love and will inhabit the same life.

I first wrestled with the dilemma of accountability and forgiveness at a Faith at Work seminar. Not only were a majority of the participants divorced; so were four of the six leaders. They created a warm, forgiving fellowship desperately needed by hurting people who had received lots of rejection from other Christians. The healing process was beautiful to see, yet I felt a vague unease. Where was the voice of commitment, exhortation, responsibility? There was deep sharing of hurt received, but little discussion of trauma inflicted on others. Was the group in danger of moving from the tough love of Christ to a sloppy agape with no absolutes? I never resolved the question at the gathering, but I've come to realize that almost every close relationship gets stretched out over the tension between uncompromising standards on the one hand and unconditional acceptance on the other. If there isn't much struggle, there probably isn't much closeness either. In fact I think many folks avoid intimacy because they tacitly understand that closeness requires both accountability and forgiveness.

Jesus had the issue forced upon him by the Pharisees when they brought before him the woman taken in adultery (Jn 8). How would he balance the demands of justice and love? His solution was to hate sin yet love the sinner. "Neither do I condemn you" were his words of assurance which preceded the warning, "Go now and leave your life of sin." Jesus didn't let the uncaring judgment of the religious pros carry the day, but neither did he give permission to sin up a storm so that grace might abound. Instead he showed a divine balancing act that all of us find hard to follow. No one ever said it would be easy.

This chapter will investigate these crucial twin topics: first accountability, then forgiveness. Although the treatments are separate, it's not without reason that I've lumped them together in the same chapter. Deep human relationships require a large dollop of both. As fallible men and women we need the counsel and encouragement of others to do what is right. As sinful men and women we need understanding and forgiveness when we invariably disappoint ourselves and the very ones we care about most.

Accountability

Late in the seventies I attended a one-week seminar on the Christian and poverty. It was held in the city where my friend Lee went to grad school. As I read the handouts and heard the lectures I was bowled over by the scriptural support for the central premise of each session—that God has a special concern for the poor. After the second day I urged Lee to attend with me. She too became convinced of God's identification with those on the margins of society.[2] In the weeks following the seminar we'd talk on the phone, encouraging each other to grow stronger in our new commitment. I got good at saying all the right words. Then one night she interrupted me midsentence: "I like what I'm hearing, Em. But what have you _done_ about it?"

Ouch. Everybody needs one friend who will keep him honest—just one. I'm not sure I could handle many more. We agreed that we both needed to have some hands-on contact with the poor. When I was little, my mom, wanting me to eat all the food on my plate, would admonish me to "think of the starving kids in China." "Name two!" was my unspoken comeback. Now as an adult I found myself in my mom's position: I had a growing concern for God's poor in the abstract, yet didn't know any personally. It took a friend's sharp words to bring me to action. We agreed that within a month we'd both hook up with a direct effort to help people—real individuals with names—break out of poverty. And we did.

"Faithful are the wounds of a friend" (Prov 27:6). That thought is built into the novel _Godric_ by my favorite Christian author, Fred Buechner. The friendship between Godric, an eleventh-century hermit, and Mouse, a lusty sea captain, is both close and turbulent. After one confrontation Godric muses, "What's friendship, when all's done, but the giving and taking of wounds."[3] Another piece of literature echoes this point. Saint-Exupery's

The Little Prince contains an account of the deepening relationship between the lonely prince and a fox. The fox refers to the bonding process as "taming." Before he departs the fox reminds the little Prince of the cost of friendship. "You become responsible, forever, for what you have tamed."[4]

To recognize our accountability to each other is one thing. To exercise it in an appropriate way is another. The line between helping a friend through a dynamic intervention and just being a plain old busybody is sometimes hard to see. You might consider the following guidelines. They've served me well over time.

1. _Win the right to be heard._ I have no warrant to go crashing into someone else's life unless I've built up the acceptance capital that friendship accumulates. I think of a time when one of our kids was at a crisis point which became semipublic knowledge. A fellow teacher was all over me with probing questions and pointed advice. My pleas for privacy were brushed aside as he stalked his prey. No way did we have the kind of relationship that would support what I regarded as pure and simple nosiness. Yet I took the same words from a close friend of long standing. His thoughts stung and gave cause for pause—but they didn't bankrupt our friendship. We both had too much invested. Hard as it was to hear his admonition, he had won both the right and the duty to give it. Unfortunately some folks are so afraid of running the relational account dry that they never use their acceptance credits for the other person's benefit. That's a loss that's hard to recoup.

2. _Contract for negative feedback._ All of us enter into relationships where we agree to hear the down side. Usually both parties recognize the obligation. An employee knows his boss has the right to hold him to performance standards. An athlete expects the coach to evaluate his play. Following scriptural precepts, some close-knit churches exercise active discipline over their members. Those that choose to belong to these churches are contracting for accountability.

Institutional reproof is much more formalized than the constructive criticism that crops up in close friendship. Few of us have the intensity of Lisa, the sensitive schizophrenic teen-ager who speaks only in rhyme in the film _David and Lisa._ She wonders what her friend David thinks of

"You have very few irritating habits, Margaret, but that is one of them."

her, and she has the courage to ask. "Look at me and what do you see?" is her open-ended invitation. Close friendship gives that opening every now and then. So does marriage.

There's a joke about a woman who complained to another couple at a dinner party that her husband never helped with day-to-day housekeeping chores. "Nonsense!" said her mate, "I do it all the time. I'll even help in the kitchen right now." His wife took him up on the offer and asked him to bring in some ice water. After five minutes he appeared in the doorway empty-handed. "Darling," he asked sheepishly, "where do we keep the water?"

I like that story. It points up the simple fact that we don't always live as we ought. I heard it from a young bride who used it as a not-so-subtle device to let her husband know she thought he wasn't doing enough around the home. It's too bad she had to resort to indirection. Intimacy gives both parties the right to say what they see.

I'm not convinced, however, that being a Christian automatically conveys the right to determine God's will for fellow believers. Some saints have so little confidence in God's sovereignty that they feel the only way others will take the right course is through their counsel and pressure. Better that we wait till asked; that way we know there's a market for our insights.

3. *Prevent gross evil.* It may have occurred to you that the two standards I've presented up to now could allow great harm to be committed without a word of protest. Suppose I see a man doing violence to a fellow human being. Don't I have both a right and a duty to speak out, even though he cares for neither me nor my opinion? The Nazi persecution of the Jews is an obvious case in point. The answer, of course, is yes. I dare not keep silent when an innocent victim suffers. This is true whether the pain is physical, emotional or spiritual. Scripture makes it clear that we should work to keep others from causing a weaker brother to stumble (Rom 14:21).

Jesus' statement about the millstone alternative to leading children astray leaves no doubt that we're to intervene when the powerless are about to get it in the neck. But there's a problem with the way many Christians apply this precept. They assume their particular Christian sensitivity should be normative for all. When faced with behavior or ideas different from their own, they are quick to cry foul. They claim that the other person might cause them to stumble. Of course they don't really see themselves as "weaker brothers" in danger of being tripped up. Wanting to be surrounded by one's own version of the truth is a natural desire. But it's not sufficient justification to crash into another's world and pop his balloon.

So when do we speak out and when do we stand mute? To me, it makes sense to adopt the traditional basketball guideline—no harm, no foul. As long as words or deeds aren't victimizing someone who can't defend herself, I keep my own counsel. If, however, there is "clear and present danger" of great harm for a defenseless person, I draw forth whatever courage I can muster and speak out.

Perhaps two borderline examples will help. I once encountered a lady with an out-of-sorts three-year-old in the supermarket. The boy was lying flat on the floor, bawling his eyes out. His mother scolded him crossly, "Act your age!" As the father of two children, it struck me that that's precisely what the kid was doing. I winced as she jerked him to his feet and spanked him sharply. It's not the way I'd discipline, but then I'm not positive that her way of doing it was worse than my way of not doing it. Before intervening I'd better be sure that the harm I'm preventing is great. I wasn't, so I bought my apples and left.

"Ever have one of those days when you felt you just had to rebuke someone?"

Two weeks later in the store's parking lot I saw three high-school guys taunting a man who's our local male version of a shopping-bag lady. He's very strange, but harmless. The same could not be said for the words of ridicule the boys were heaping on him. Ordinarily I'd have no reservation about calling a halt to such fun. It was a tougher decision that time because two of the guys had begun to come to my Young Life club and hear the claims of the Christian message. Would my intervention drive them away? Still, trying to save a helpless person from unnecessary hurt seems to be at the core of the gospel as I know it, so I stepped in. No, the boys never came back to the club.

4. _Confront in private._ "A friend is one who stands up for you in public and sits down on you in private."[5] I like that. I've benefited from this approach when my wife has found it necessary to admonish me. Once after church we were standing around talking, and I was ready to make some cutting remark about an individual. Jeanie saw it coming and unobtrusively placed the heel of her shoe on my instep. Later in private we talked through the issue. I was much more open to changing future behavior because I hadn't lost face in front of others. Like the principle of preventing harm to an innocent person, this principle has solid biblical roots (Mt 18:15-17). Public confrontation is an avenue of last resort. One-on-one private consultation is the preferred route.

As I'm writing this, American hostages are being released from Lebanon after their week-long hijacking ordeal on a TWA flight. It wasn't the "bomb-the-stew-out-of-them" rhetoric that achieved their freedom; it was behind-the-scenes negotiation. Some people get their jollies by public posturing of righteous indignation. They feel better, but the situation gets worse. The question can often be reduced to a matter of what you want most. If you want the rush that comes from sounding the alarm—go public. If your aim is to help the offending individual change his or her behavior—stay private.

5. _Ask, don't announce._ Tentativeness is often more persuasive than certainty. This is especially true when it comes to holding others accountable to their own standards. Early in my Young Life work I became concerned that I not lure kids into easy-believism. I wanted them to understand that although accepting God's love is a simple act, it has long-term implications for how we live. I had a list of nonnegotiables that I'm embarrassed to present here—so I won't. Suffice it to say that every teen-ager under my sway was told in no uncertain terms what his conduct should be.

Over time I developed a different approach. As we went through key verses together, I presented Christ's demand that anyone wanting to follow

Drawing by Ziegler; © 1984 The New Yorker Magazine, Inc.

"I'm sorry, Timmy, but you are wrong. You are terribly, terribly wrong."

him must "take up his cross daily" (Lk 9:23). I then asked them to tell me what this might mean for their lives. Of course the responses varied, but on the whole these about-to-be-Christians came up with a much more detailed and significant cluster of changes than I would have worked out for them. I listened to them and believed them. I also saw them become more Christlike in their actions than the kids who had heard my edicts. Whether this was because my new approach made them less defensive or because they knew better than I the sore spots of their lives, I'm not sure. But the results made me a believer in such tentative words as *maybe, perhaps* and *possibly*.

Tentativeness isn't just a technique. It's an attitude that's very close to the biblical virtue of humility. As fallen and raised members of the human race, we're really all on the same level. In our achievements we're all laymen in every area except one. I can give a good public speech without getting flustered. People don't fall asleep, and they usually go away knowing and considering what I've said. But lest I get cocky, let me add that I can't read an income statement like my accountant, tune an engine like my mechanic, or read the original Hebrew and Greek texts of Scripture like my colleagues in the Bible department. As a matter of fact I'm a complete bust in these areas.

The same principle holds in moral conduct. I may not do what you do that displeases God, but I have my own packet of sins with which to grapple. Even if I look better than another in some area, I know down deep that there but for the grace of God go I. Does all this mean I have no warrant to point out God's best for others? By no means. It does mean, however, that we seek to help each other in a spirit of mutuality. Neither of us is "one up" on the other. My urgings to you today make your insights for me tomorrow even more appropriate. Together we may be able to fill in the gaps.

I'm not convinced the world needs more prophets. In God's economy the shoot-from-the-hip, lay-waste-the-town brand of judgment seems to predate Jesus' appearance on earth. But we still need the gentle nudges of those who have won the right to mirror back our lives. It's risky. If we don't encourage others to do it, they may get scared off. I recall the time in our marriage when I got tired of trying to guess what Jeanie wanted. I told her I was a lousy mind reader and would appreciate her simply telling me what she desired. I'll never forget her response—"But if I tell you, you might not give it." The same is true when we point out areas to change. After doing it just right, we still may end up having our words ignored and our persons rejected. But as I told Jeanie, consider the alternative. Mankind is plagued with lots of body-at-rest inertia. If we don't ever share our insights, we're robbing our friends of a chance to change.

There's one final requirement for the kind of straight talk I'm advocating. We should never call on friends to clean up their act in the future if we aren't willing to forgive their actions of the past. People change only when there's hope of a better life. It would be cruel indeed to call for change without also offering the possibility of forgiveness. Accountability and forgiveness go hand in hand.

Forgiveness

I ran into Larry at the Seven Dwarfs restaurant. It had been about that many years since we'd sat face to face. I had warm memories of our families' spending two vacations together—especially fun times because Jeanie and I knew of no other couple as positive toward life and vibrant in the faith as Larry and Susan. Then somehow Susan "outgrew" the husband of her youth. Larry was stifling her personal growth. She no longer valued his optimism and hearty cheerfulness. She had an affair with another man and sought a divorce. Larry hung on for three years, but the coldness of one-way love took its toll and they finally split. Anger, bitterness and disillusionment became his new companions. He was devastated.

In his marvelous book, *Forgive and Forget*, Lew Smedes has labeled forgiveness the "hardest trick in the whole bag of personal relationships."[6] It is an outrage against all natural sensibilities. It's only by faith that we can see the Old Testament prophet Hosea as a model of unconditional divine love and not some neurotic masochist. To forgive is to perform spiritual surgery on the soul. Every act of forgiveness is truly a miracle.

Somehow Larry pulled it off. Seated across from my luncheon special was a man who could speak of his former wife without gagging on the soup. Not only was he in regular contact with her because of their kids, he had the power to wish her well in her new marriage.

Make no mistake. Larry still defines his abandonment as an act of disloyalty if not outright betrayal. He doesn't lessen its horror in order to excuse it, lower his standards for marriage in order to tolerate it or blur its memory in order to forget it. But there came a time when he decided that as delicious as hate is, the accompanying bile of indigestion was poisoning the rest of his life. He concluded with Hannah Arendt that "the only remedy for the inevitability of our history is forgiveness." So as much for his own sake as for hers, Larry forgave Susan.

I wonder if she knows? From Larry's standpoint the process of forgiveness followed the pattern that Smedes sets forth: first *hurt*, then *hate*, followed by *healing* and finally *coming together*.[7] That's history. But forgiveness is ultimately a receiver variable. Has Susan experienced the fresh breeze of forgiveness? Many haven't.

There's a poignant story about a father who wanted to reconcile with his estranged son. The man posted this notice in the town's public square:

Son—all is forgiven.

Meet me here Sunday at sunset.

Seventy-five young men showed up.

That image haunts me. Are there folks out there still feeling a load of guilt long after it's been lifted? They're forgiven, but they don't feel it. In my best academic fashion I did a computer search to locate research on interpersonal forgiveness, pardon and reconciliation. Almost nothing was there. The world doesn't think in these categories. So I decided to run a simple study on the communication of forgiveness.[8] I wanted to find out what things make a person feel forgiven and what responses drive the wooden stake of guilt into the heart.

I started by locating twenty people who were good candidates for forgiveness. I used Smedes's criteria: they had to have hurt another person deeply and unfairly. I think I succeeded. The people I found included:

☐ A church secretary who violated the pastor's confidence by repeating to a church member a negative statement the minister had made about him.

"Frankly, Cleo, I'm more hurt than angry."

☐ A college student who had secretly copied his roommate's take-home test; the professor spotted the similarities and lowered both grades.

☐ A fellow who seduced a girl and then dumped her; felt lonely and resumed their intimacy; then dropped her again.

☐ A guy who, when he became interested in a girl, ignored his best friend.

☐ A daughter who came home from college and disavowed to their faces everything her parents believed and stood for.

☐ A writer who discredited in print the life's work of his closest friend.

Half my subjects were male, half were female. Half were still in college, half were postgraduates. Half were married, half were single. They ranged in age from twenty to fifty. All of them came out of an evangelical tradition, so you'll have to decide if their experience transfers to folks of different backgrounds. You'll also need to consider whether a sample size of twenty is large enough to give meaningful results. My feeling is that these people were recounting panhuman experience. All of them had suffered deep guilt for something they had done to another. All desired forgiveness. Perhaps most important, all were willing to talk about it.

The first significant thing I discovered is that the feeling of forgiveness is an either/or experience. I had all twenty indicate on a ten-point scale to what extent they felt forgiven by the person they'd hurt. Fourteen of the twenty used the top end of the scale: 8, 9 or 10. The average was 9.5. Obviously these people were confident that they'd been pardoned. The other six responded at the low end: 1, 2 or 3. The average was 2.0. These folks were certain that the victim continued to bear ill will toward them. There was no middle ground. No one gave a response of 4, 5, 6 or 7. Apparently forgiveness is a dichotomous variable. You either feel it or you don't. Either way, you're sure.

The Way We Were

As I played with the data of the study I was reminded of the dreaded card in childhood Monopoly games: "Go directly to jail. Do not pass Go. Do not collect $200." That's nonforgiveness. Normal life ceases. No rides on the Reading. No strolls on the Boardwalk. No opportunities to take a Chance.

"We used to be close friends as well as good neighbors. Almost every evening, we enjoyed the sunset together, philosophizing about this and that. Then, one day, we had a slight difference, and ever since then he's tried to spoil this wonderful moment."

When normal activities cease, we feel locked off in a corner. Conversely, when we get back to the familiar routine, we feel forgiven. We shake the dice, move our marker, pay rent, buy property, make deals. Things are like they used to be. We're back to Go.

This return to normal life may be an illusion. Logic tells us that life can never be quite the same after monumental hurt. Even if the wound has healed, there's still scar tissue. But the more the present mirrors the past, the greater the assurance of pardon. As one participant in the study said with great relief, "Things are now back where they used to be." "Seems Like Old Times" is not only a song title. It's the fervent hope of all who desire forgiveness.

I'm reminded of a scene in the gripping movie _Country_. A farm family is caught in the crunch of higher seed and fertilizer costs and lower prices for their crops. The farmer cracks under the pressure of impending foreclosure. He abandons the livestock, gets drunk and strikes his son. Days later husband, wife and son are standing together in the kitchen for the first time since the blowup. They eye each other warily. Then the grandfather walks in, sizes up the situation and briskly announces: "Tell you what I'm going to do. I'm going to make myself a pot of coffee . . . stand by the sink and drink it like I usually do . . . and when I'm done I'm going to my place, light a fire, maybe read a little, then I'm going to bed. In the morning I'm goin' on about my business."⁹

Business as usual. Things are back to normal. It's quite comforting.

Beg Your Pardon

There's a great debate among writers on forgiveness concerning the necessity of repentance.¹⁰ Is forgiveness conditional? Does the violator have to apologize to the victim to be absolved? Before you answer that question for yourself, I caution you to remember that we aren't speaking in theological terms. We're talking about mending human rifts, not cosmic separation.

My conclusion is that it's possible to forgive an unrepentant offender. Not easy, but possible. If it weren't, we'd be condemned to tote around a gunnysack of bitterness. Some people never repent. Others die or move away before they have a chance to express their sorrow. But that's the _fact_ of forgiveness. How about the _feeling_? Here it's a different story.

All fourteen folks who felt forgiven in my study had made some kind of apology to the persons they'd hurt. Sometimes it took only a simple, "I'm sorry." More often it involved a tearful communication of distress over the hurt caused. In almost every case the apology was coupled with stated intent not to repeat the offense. Apparently offenders need to make a confession and a promise before they can allow themselves to shuck a load of guilt. Forgiveness may not require repentance. Face-to-face reconciliation does.

The two-way transaction of forgiveness is beautifully captured by Frederick Buechner:

© Punch—ROTHCO

COTHAM

"Roll down the window, James, apologize profusely to all concerned and then move on!"

To forgive somebody is to say one way or another, "You have done something unspeakable, and by all rights I should call it quits between us. Both my pride and my principles . . . demand no less. However, although I make no guarantees that I will be able to forget what you've done and though we may both carry the scars for life, I refuse to let it stand between us. I still want you for my friend."

To accept forgiveness means to admit that you've done something unspeakable that needs to be forgiven, and thus both parties must swallow the same thing: their pride. . . .

When you forgive somebody who has wronged you, you're spared the dismal corrosion of bitterness and wounded pride.

For both parties, forgiveness means the freedom again to be at peace inside their own skins and to be glad in each other's presence.[11]

The Sounds of Silence

Judgment is pronounced when the person who's been hurt cuts off communication. No other finding came through so clearly: silence equals condemnation. Communication, by contrast, equals forgiveness.

The fellow who had his test copied didn't speak to his roommate for two months. The twice-abandoned girl would respond only if the guy agreed to marry her. Offenders were left dangling when the person they'd hurt wouldn't look them in the eye, returned notes unopened, gave them the cold shoulder. Some who spoke gave only monosyllabic responses.

"How are you feeling today?"

"Fine."

"Is anything wrong?"

"No."

One wounded person told a mutual friend, "I never want to hear her name mentioned again."

The beginning of communication signaled the start of forgiveness. The cold winter of judgment was over. The spring thaw of pardon had begun. The persons who had been betrayed had to initiate the dialog—it was their move. Subjects reported the relief they felt when they received that first note, phone call or knock on the door. Long walks and long talks were cherished as valuable in their own right. It made little difference what was said. The mere fact of communication spoke volumes.

Calling up memories of happier times seems to be especially healing. The fond recollection of earlier incidents creates a secondhand reality. The past is overlaid on the present, assuring the offender that all is forgiven.

Benign Neglect

There's one exception to the communication = forgiveness equation. If I've hurt you, I dread hearing you talk of the unspeakable act that I performed. Of course it has to come up once to clear the air. If it's never mentioned, the offense will lurk behind every utterance and poison the relationship further. But once confronted, I don't want you to bring it up again. Recurring references solidify guilt.

Many respondents noted that the other person never referred to the offense again. The pastor confronted the loose-tongued secretary immediately, but that was the only time he ever spoke of her indiscretion. A mother was deeply grieved when the police came to the house to arrest her son. But after the initial shock she treated him as if nothing had happened.

Obviously people who were hurt recall the event. But by not giving voice to these memories they cooperate in a kind of benign conspiracy. As Paul suggests, they are "forgetting what is behind and straining toward to what is ahead" (Phil 3:13). In this way they edit their memories so that one blow to the foundations of their relationship does not turn into repeated blows that eventually demolish the whole structure.

Two people in the study recalled that the hurt person referred to the offense in a joking manner, probably in an effort to convert the situation into something less tragic. Mutual laughter is often a great tension reliever, and yet I can imagine the offender's laugh sounding a bit hollow. My advice to the person wanting to communicate forgiveness is to drop all discussion of the offense—even joking references. That's not avoidance. It's kindness.

Voluntary Vulnerability

I once dreamed that two wolves were engaged in what looked like a fight-to-the-death struggle. One wolf raked the other with his teeth. Although the wound was not fatal, the drawing of blood escalated the battle's frenzy. Suddenly the animal that was winning flopped over on his back and exposed his neck. This surrender tactic disarmed the wounded beast, and the fight stopped. A psychiatrist would have a field day analyzing the conflict within me that the dream portrays. But I also see it as a picture of forgiveness.

If I am unfairly wounded by another it puts me in a "one-up" moral position. I can hold this ethical club over the other indefinitely. "Don't get mad. Get even," is the world's advice to victims of injustice. Even if they refuse to extract their pound of flesh, prudence suggests they at least proceed cautiously. "Once burned, twice shy," is the pithy description of the relational situation. Or, in the words of a homespun proverb: "Fool me once, shame on you. Fool me twice, shame on me."

Flying in the face of this sound advice is the foolishness of forgiveness. Nowhere is this vulnerability seen more starkly than in the biblical account of Hosea. He marries the unfaithful Gomer and tries to make an honest woman of her. She in turn makes a mockery of his love and goes whoring after others. But the sad slob comes back for more. In the process, Gomer—

along with we who read of Hosea's vulnerability—gets a taste of true forgiveness.

The subjects in my study had lots to say about power, status and superiority. All acknowledged that their actions had put them in a morally inferior position. When the hurt party voluntarily stepped down from the one-up position, the offenders saw it as a clear sign of forgiveness. Of course it didn't always happen.

One fellow felt the other had permanently relegated him to the status of second-class citizen. Another noted a condescending attitude that sneered, "I'm sorry for you way down there." The best friend who was replaced by a girl brought up the theological big guns. "You're choosing second best," he charged. "Until you repent of this you're out of God's will."

But not all victims used their superior moral ground to hold down the offender. Like the wolf of my fantasy, some gave the other a second chance to hurt them. The pastor shared other confidences. The man whose work was called into question gave his writer friend permission to publish future anecdotes. Many continued to disclose their innermost thoughts. As one girl said, "I felt forgiven because she shared her feelings."

Voluntary vulnerability is a way of displaying equal regard. It acknowledges the truth that we all have the capacity to be friend or fiend—and that the two aren't far apart. The hurt person looks at the one who's done the wrong and says, "There, but for the grace of God, go I." This attitude sees Hosea neither as a neurotic masochist or a spineless wimp, but as one who lovingly communicates forgiveness.

Show Me

In "Show Me," a song from the musical _My Fair Lady,_ Eliza Doolittle sings of her frustration at expressions of love limited to mere words: "Don't talk of June! Don't talk of fall! Don't talk at all! Show me."[12]

That could be the theme song of candidates for forgiveness. Although some heard the statement, "I forgive you," the words themselves had little impact. Offenders looked for confirmation in deeds. If the victim's response mirrored reconciliation, the assurance of pardon was unnecessary. In chapter seven I presented three responses that heightened attraction: paying compliments, giving and accepting favors and exchanging touch. The same three factors are crucial in showing forgiveness.

People in my study felt off the hook when the folks they hurt paid them _compliments_. The guy who had his test stolen praised his roommate's athletic ability. The pastor spoke highly in public about his secretary's work. The parents bragged about their daughter. The man whose effectiveness was called into question complimented the writer on being a loving husband. Note that all these positive strokes were outside the realm of the offense. But no difference. Any sort of compliment was taken as a sign that forgiveness was present. Nice words in one area blanketed the whole relationship.

People who feel guilty often try to get back in the good graces of others by doing _favors_. The men and women I interviewed were no exception. Their attempts at reconciliation included washing cars, cleaning apartments, sending candy and lending money. When their efforts were accepted with appreciation, they believed that relational peace had been restored. But sometimes their efforts were rebuffed. Victims seemed to understand that any acceptance of a kindness would signal de facto forgiveness. So presents were returned unopened, and offers of help were refused. These cold responses signaled the continuance of interpersonal tension.

Favors can also work the other way. When the person who's been treated badly goes out of her way to do something nice for the offender, it's a token of forgiveness. Despite being blasted by their daughter, the girl's parents continued to pay for school. Not surprisingly she felt like fellowship was re-established. Most favors that were reported to me were on a much smaller scale: buying an ice cream cone, helping with homework, coming to a track meet. They're all little things, but when you're hurting, little things mean a lot.

On the basis of my interviews I can say with certainty that no single act communicates forgiveness with such certainty as intentional _touch_. Other nonverbal means can be effective—an encouraging smile, a friendly wave. But a squeeze of the hand, a playful punch, a back rub or especially a warm hug are unmistakable. Their presence dissolves guilt. Their absence calls into question any other indication of pardon. It's lousy poetry but sound advice:

If you forgive them much,
Don't cause them to clutch—
Convey pardon and such
By touch.

All Wounds Take Time

A few years ago I hurt someone bad. What was worse, I was so insensitive that I didn't even know I'd wounded my friend until a third party clued me in. As soon as I realized what had happened I rushed out to apologize. I felt awful and wanted instant forgiveness. That wasn't wrong—just dumb. "Time heals all wounds," they say. As is often the case, "they" are partially wrong. It's not as automatic as the slogan suggests, but it's true that any gash in a relationship takes time to mend. This was borne out time and time again by those in my study. In fact, some are still waiting for the wounds to heal.

At the start of this discussion I referred to Smedes's four steps toward forgiveness. I think this is an accurate way of diagramming them:

Hurt —► Hate ——————————————► Forgive —►Come Together

Hate follows on the heels of hurt. But forgiveness takes time for both parties to master. It's a shame we have to wait so long, but then it's a shame the hurt occurred in the first place. Waiting for forgiveness is hard, but it's better than the alternative.

This past year a man I like and respect called me to account for my actions within an organization. Although I'm convinced that what I did was proper and aboveboard, I also know that I'm capable of self-deception. He was right in raising the issue. Behavior that has a lasting impact on others' lives ought to be open to scrutiny. Unfortunately he announced his condemnation, without prior warning, in a public forum.

I was stunned. There was no tentativeness to the judgment, no spirit of inquiry. The surprise nature of the censure offered me no opportunity to prepare a response. Like the quarterback blindsided by the blitzing line-backer, I never saw it coming. I was embarrassed and confused, and I felt a deep sense of shame. Hate came later.

So did forgiveness. More for my sake than his I had to find a way to get rid of bitterness. If it relieved him of guilt in the process, so much the better. The findings of my forgiveness research suggested a course of action.

I started by letting him know a bit of my hurt. He agreed we'd have to get together to work it out, but months went by and nothing happened. I realized that I'd been unfair in not telling him my real agony. The guy isn't a mind reader. I also needed to make the first move at re-establishing communication.

When we met in a restaurant midway between our home cities, I spelled out my hurt. To my surprise I discovered I didn't even need an apology. I was able to regard my colleague as a fellow struggler in the quest to act honorably without hearing "I'm sorry." I did hear that, however, along with a promise to avoid a repeat performance. We spent our final hour planning how to work together in the future. A hug seemed more appropriate than a handshake when we parted. The meeting lasted two hours, but the internal process took five months. You can't rush forgiveness.

Accountability and forgiveness make our friendships grow and mature. Many relationships never progress past the diaper stage because one or both parties are afraid to say the hard word in love. That's too bad. Accountability was given to us so we'd get better. Forgiveness was given to us for fun.

10

THE FRIENDSHIP MANDATE

Communication = Content + Relationship

THROUGHOUT THESE PAGES you've encountered Gordon, Bill, Lee, Bruce, Melinda and John. What do they have in common? In various ways all of them help Em Griffin feel good about himself. Wonders of wonders, I seem to do the same for them. They are friends.

Does the certainty of that open claim leave you uneasy? It may; the world is uncomfortable with intimacy apart from romance. C. S. Lewis notes that there are myriads of poems about romantic attraction, but no ode to friendship. He thinks that's because so few have it.[1]

There's something blatantly undemocratic about friendship. To announce, "You are my friend!" to someone, is to say by implication to another, "You are not." Thomas Jefferson's original draft of the Declaration of Independence stated that our Republic was built on friendship, but he subsequently removed the words when others were threatened by the idea.

As a teacher I find myself ill at ease when facing two students who have a special bond. Their knowing looks and bursts of unexpected laughter

**"The sad part of being a dictator is that one has so few close friends
and those few have to be watched very carefully."**

make it clear that I'm an outsider to their private world. I self-consciously
begin to watch my words. I also make sure all my buttons are buttoned and
zippers are zipped. Somehow their closeness seems a threat to my authority.

Revolutionary leaders lash out against private ties. They want followers
to sacrifice everything for the cause, and intimacy between two persons
might endanger the solidarity of the group. Business leaders expect similar
loyalty to the company. Friendliness is a corporate asset; friendship is not.
It's not without reason that some employees of IBM think the letters stand

Cartoon by Scott. Appeared in *Saturday Review*, April 17, 1976.

"Fourteen people love me, 22 people like me, 6 people tolerate me,
and I have only 3 enemies. Not bad for a little kid, huh?"

for "I've been moved." A policy of frequent transfers inhibits the development of relationships that might drain energy from bottom-line enhancement.

Friendship is downplayed in other, more subtle ways. We expect that immature kids will speak of playmates, friends and cliques, but grown-ups are supposed to put that behind them as they get on with matters of consequence. The adult view seems to be that friends are a nice add-on, but aren't necessary to the stuff of real life. If young singles are questioned about possible romantic interest in another, they're likely to say with a shrug, "Aw, we're just friends." Why *just?* Why would friendship be of lesser magnitude than romance? Because the average person doesn't know how magnitude than romance? Because the average person doesn't know how to handle intimacy. In most fellowships, friendship is still a deviant activity.

Despite this discomfort, friendship for the Christian is not an option. It's a mandate! Near the end of his ministry, Jesus told his disciples: "I no longer call you servants, because a servant does not know his master's business. Instead, I have called you friends, for everything that I have learned from my Father I have made known to you" (Jn 15:15).

I had always regarded servanthood as God's highest calling for us. But Jesus upgraded the relationship. No longer servants—friends! Note that he didn't say that to everyone, just the Twelve. He played favorites. He was especially close to Peter, James and John. And of these three, John alone referred to himself as "the disciple whom he loved" (Jn 19:26). That may seem a bit arrogant, but of what can a man boast if not his friends? Jesus' words and example make it plain that we are spiritually impoverished if we don't have at least one or two soul friends.

There's a theological reason for placing a high priority on friendship. The Incarnation isn't over. When we ask Jesus to come into our life, he really does. "You   have clothed yourself with Christ," as Paul says (Gal 3:27). Christ in us is our "hope of glory" (Col 1:27). Therefore when people get to know us, they're also drawing closer to the Savior. "What a friend we have in Jesus," we sing with confidence. But the reverse is also true—what a Jesus we have in friends!

I'm firmly committed to an orthodox Christian stand—the faith that God has "once for all entrusted to the saints" (Jude 3). Yet one Christian writer contends that true orthodoxy consists of more than just correct doctrine or right belief.[2] Scriptural fidelity also requires quality relationships.

Friendship is terminal. I don't mean it will kill you, though sometimes it feels like it. I mean that friendship is an end in itself. That's a rather radical thought in today's society where folks tend to love things and use people. But humans aren't supposed to be used. "Use things and love people" has it right. The Jewish theologian Martin Buber gives a solemn warning: "One cannot divide one's life between an actual relationship to God and an inactual I-It relationship to the world—praying to God in truth

"Mr. Carver is out. This is his best friend."

and utilizing the world. Whoever knows the world as something to be utilized knows God the same way."[3]

The relationship between David and Jonathan is a beautiful model of an I-Thou bond. "Jonathan became one in spirit with David, and he loved him as himself" (1 Sam 18:1). Perhaps these men inspired the description in Ecclesiastes 4:9-12: "Two are better than one, because they have a good return for their work. If one falls down, his friend can help him up. But pity the man who falls and has no one to help him up! Also, if two lie down together, they will keep warm. But can one keep warm alone? Though one may be overpowered, two can defend themselves."

While claiming neither the love for God nor the domestic turmoil these two men had, I'm aware that close friendships have helped me survive a number of life's blows. Others note that too. Every once in a while I get together with three colleagues for a long Saturday breakfast. We were sharing some crises each of us faced when one guy asked me: "Em, you've had to face a number of personal traumas, yet you don't seem to get thrown for a loop. How come?"

Before I could respond, another fellow jumped in and said, "It's because Em has chosen to build a network of friends that give his life stability." He's right—not only about the network, but about the fact that it was built through conscious choice.

Today I choose to be with friends. As I write this paragraph I'm on an airplane speeding toward Chicago. Later today the Chicago Bears play in their first Super Bowl. This may not mean much to readers in another time and another place, but to this victory-starved Chicago sports fan it ranks just behind my twenty-fifth anniversary celebration as a signal event to savor with friends. As one of the TV commercials during a time-out will state, "It doesn't get any better than this."

The ad has it only half right, however. It would have us believe that this special camaraderie comes only through beer talk with the boys. Footing the bill of a million dollars per minute may give them the right to make this claim, but intimate bonds are available to nondrinkers and women as well. My research among best friends showed only a few discrepancies among friendship types. Male friendships were harder to come by but had longer lasting stability once formed. Intimate female bonds formed more easily, but women seemed to have less control over the future of their relationship. Romantic couples showed the physical affection we'd expect, and cross-sex platonic pairs proved more volatile. Despite these differences, I found a common thread of friendship weaving all intimate relationships into a single cloth.[4]

This conclusion isn't based on one isolated study among students at a Christian college. Extensive research has identified a whole cluster of goodies that typify close friendship: enjoyment, acceptance, trust, respect, mutual assistance, confiding, understanding and spontaneity.[5] Romance is marked by all these characteristics, and adds passion and exclusiveness. As C. S. Lewis notes, friends sit side by side, their gaze on a common goal.

Lovers sit face to face with eyes fixed on each other.[6]

It strikes me that any of the characteristics of friendship is worth the price of admission. Taken together, they offer a human pearl of great value that makes the field cheap at any price. I'm not the only one to feel that way. Consider Fred Buechner's description of the self-confirmation that came from his first close relationship away from home: "It was Jimmy who became my great friend, and it was through coming to know him that I discovered that perhaps I was not, as I had always suspected, alone in the universe and the only one of my kind. He was another who saw the world enough as I saw it to make me believe that maybe it was the way the world actually was."[7]

There are risks, of course. Initial rejection or a later falling-out loom as ever-present possibilities. This whole book is an attempt to lengthen the odds against disaster, but it could happen. Perhaps my background prepared me to take the chance. My father encouraged me to adopt a gambling spirit that sought to beat the odds. "Bet big to win big" was his motto. When it comes to friends, that's good advice.

Embarrassment is certain. To reach the bonding levels of intimacy, it is not enough to speak of the self or even of the other. The relationship itself must be aired. It's possible to overtalk a friendship—paralysis by analysis. But occasional deep communication is necessary for increasing closeness.[8] And frankly, it's sometimes embarrassing to discuss us. I know of no way around this hurdle. Just as our individual lives have passages that need to be marked by celebration and reflection, so do our friendships. As the old joke goes, if we find birthdays bothersome, consider the alternative.

Friendship takes time. It's impossible to develop an in-depth relationship with the collector at a toll booth, at least during working hours. No matter how great the quality of interaction, without a quantity of time together, coldness advances. And mere time is also insufficient. I can be thrown together with someone eight hours a day, five days a week and still remain distant. It's when I freely choose to squander hours with another that I feed our friendship. The best thing to spend on a friend is time.

Every month I ride the train to downtown Chicago and meet a man who is too busy. We sit all afternoon in a deserted restaurant talking of our

When you have a friend, you have everything.

families, our work, our faith, our passions, our fears and, yes, our relationship. I don't have time for this, and neither does he. Yet we are at each other's disposal. The very difficulty of wrenching time out of busy schedules makes our friendship more valuable.

Lost time, embarrassment, possible rejection—these are the risks of intimacy. They strike me as rather low-grade risks when compared to the benefits.

An intimate friendship has a life of its own that is greater than the separate lives of the two friends. The spiritual child called friendship is born from the love two people have for each other. As with physical children, the birth of a spiritual child is no accident. The way it grows is no mystery. The choice facing potential parents is clear. On one side is contraception, abortion and desertion. On the other is the nurturing that leads to intimacy with all its uncertainties, risks and hurts. I opt for intimacy.

Teilhard de Chardin once said: "Someday, after we have mastered the winds and the waves, the tides, and gravity, we will harness for God the energies of love, and then for the second time in the history of the world man will have discovered fire."[9]

I say, "Why wait!"

Notes

Introduction
[1]Em Griffin, *The Mind Changers* (Wheaton, Ill.: Tyndale, 1976).
[2]Em Griffin, *Getting Together* (Downers Grove, Ill.: InterVarsity Press, 1982).
[3]I'd like to thank Court Burkhart who aided in the selection of the cartoons.

Chapter 1: The Rules of the Game
[1]Dean C. Barnlund, "Toward a Meaning-Centered Philosophy of Communication," *Journal of Communication* 12 (1962): 197-211.
[2]Judy C. Pearson, *Interpersonal Communication* (Glenview, Ill.: Scott Foresman, 1983), p. 7.
[3]This is my paraphrase of the underlying basis for the research of David McClelland. See David McClelland, *Human Motivation* (Glenview, Ill.: Scott Foresman, 1985), pp. v-vii.
[4]Charles R. Berger and Richard J. Calabrese, "Some Explorations in Initial Interaction and Beyond: Towards A Developmental Theory of Interpersonal Communication," *Human Communication Research* 1 (1975): 99-112.
[5]Dan P. Millar and Frank E. Millar, *Messages and Myths* (New York: Alfred Publishing, 1976), pp. 29-46.
[6]Paul Watzlawick, Janet Beavin and Don Jackson, *Pragmatics of Human Communication* (New York: W. W. Norton, 1967), pp. 48-50.
[7]Kenneth Burke, *A Rhetoric of Motives* (New York: Prentice-Hall, 1950), p. 22.
[8]John Powell, *Why Am I Afraid to Tell You Who I Am?* (Niles, Ill.: Argus Communications, 1969), p. 69.
[9]Barnlund, "Toward A Meaning-Centered Philosophy," pp. 197-211.
[10]Watzlawick, Beavin and Jackson, *Pragmatics of Human Communication*, p. 51.
[11]Loraine Halfen Zephyr, "Creating Your Spiritual Child," in *Bridges Not Walls*, 3d ed., ed. John Stewart (Reading, Mass.: Addison-Wesley, 1982), p. 34.

Chapter 2: Self-Concept

[1]Chad Gordon, "Self-Conceptions: Configurations of Content," *The Self in Social Interaction,* vol. 1, eds. Chad Gordon and Kenneth Gergen (New York: John Wiley & Sons, 1968), pp. 115-36.

[2]Abraham Maslow, *Motivation and Personality* (New York: Harper & Row, 1954), pp. 35-58.

[3]C. W. Sherif, M. Sherif and R. Nebergall, *Attitude and Attitude Change: The Social Judgment-Involvement Approach* (Philadelphia: W. B. Saunders, 1965).

[4]Erich Fromm, "The Theory of Love," from *The Art of Loving* (New York: Harper & Row, 1956), pp. 7-31.

[5]Gordon, "Self Conceptions," pp. 115-36.

[6]William James, *Psychology: The Briefer Course* (New York: Henry Holt, 1892), pp. 187-88.

[7]Donald Hayes and Leo Meltzer, "Interpersonal Judgments Based on Talkativeness," *Sociometry* 35 (1972): 538-61.

[8]Arthur Cohen, "Some Implications of Self-Esteem for Social Influence," *Self in Social Interaction,* pp. 383-84.

[9]Ibid.

[10]S. B. Kiesler and R. L. Baral, "The Search for a Romantic Partner: The Effects of Self-Esteem and Physical Attractiveness on Romantic Behavior," *Personality and Social Behavior,* eds. Kenneth Gergen and D. Marlowe (Reading, Mass.: Addison Wesley, 1970), pp. 155-65.

[11]G. Lesser and R. Abelson, "Correlates of Persuasibility In Children," *Personality and Persuasibility,* ed. C. Hovland and I. Janis (New Haven: Yale University Press, 1959), pp. 187-206.

[12]Cohen, "Implications of Self-Esteem," pp. 383-84.

[13]Kenneth Gergen, *The Concept of Self* (New York: Holt, Rinehart and Winston, 1971), pp. 66-67.

[14]"Door Interview: John Claypool," *Wittenburg Door,* April/May 1978, p. 9.

[15]Gergen, *Concept of Self,* p. 73.

[16]Charles Horton Cooley, "The Social Self: Or the Meanings of 'I,' " *Self in Social Interaction,* pp. 87-91.

[17]George Bernard Shaw, *Pygmalion, Selected Plays* (New York: Dodd Mead, 1948), p. 270.

[18]Erik H. Erikson, "Identity and Identity Diffusion," *Self in Social Interaction,* pp. 197-205.

[19]Gergen, *Concept of Self,* p. 73.

[20]Shelley Duval and Robert Wicklund, *A Theory of Objective Self-Awareness* (New York: Academic Press, 1972), p. 4.

[21]Ellen Berscheid, Elaine Walster and George Bohrnstedt, "The Happy American Body: A Survey Report," *Psychology Today,* November 1973, p. 119.

Chapter 3: Motivation

[1]Joan Whitehead, *Motivation and Learning* (Milton Keynes, England: Open Univer-

sity Press, 1976), p. 40.

[2]Viktor Frankl, *Man's Search for Meaning* (New York: Washington Square Press, 1963), p. 154.

[3]Kenneth Terhune, "Motives, Situation, and Interpersonal Conflict within A Prisoner's Dilemma," *Journal of Personality And Social Psychology* 8, Monograph supplement (1968): 1-24.

[4]The self-descriptions for nAch, nAff and nPow are taken from Griffin, *Getting Together,* pp. 43, 45.

[5]Ernest Dichter, *The Strategy of Desire* (Garden City, N.Y.: Doubleday and Co., 1960), p. 46.

[6]David McClelland and Robert Steele, *Motivation Workshops* (New York: General Learning Press, 1972), pp. 33-51. I'd like to thank Dr. McClelland for providing the stimulus picture. It is used with his permission.

[7]The interpretation of TAT results is based on the extensive discussion in David McClelland's *Human Motivation* (Glenview, Ill.: Scott Foresman, 1985). Chapters 6-9 and 13 are especially helpful.

Chapter 4: Perception

[1]John Culkin, as quoted in Edmund Carpenter, *They Became What They Beheld* (New York: Ballantine, 1970), p. 12.

[2]Hadley Cantril, "Perception and Interpersonal Relations," *American Journal of Psychiatry* 114 (1957): 125.

[3]Florence Kluckhohn and Fred Strodtbeck, *Variations in Value Orientations* (Evanston, Ill.: Row, Peterson, 1961). See chapter 1.

[4]This picture was brought to the attention of psychologists by Edward G. Boring in 1930. Created by cartoonist W. E. Hill, it was originally published in *Puck,* November 6, 1915, as "My Wife and My Mother-in-law."

[5]Gordon W. Allport and Leo F. Postman, "The Basic Psychology of Rumor," *Transactions of the New York Academy of Sciences,* Series 2, 8 (1945): 61-81.

[6]Hughes Mearns, "The Psychoed" in *Creative Power,* 2d rev. ed. (New York: Dover Publications, 1958), p. 94. Courtesy of Dover Publications.

[7]David Schneider, Albert Hastorf and Phebe Ellsworth, *Person Perception,* 2d ed. (Reading, Mass.: Addison-Wesley Publishing Co., 1979), p. 77.

[8]Ibid., pp. 182-83.

[9]L. Robert Kohls, *Survival Kit for Overseas Living* (Chicago: Intercultural Press, 1979), p. 73.

[10]David Myers, *The Human Puzzle* (New York: Harper & Row, 1978), p. 250.

[11]Chaim Potok, *The Chosen* (New York: Simon and Schuster, 1967), pp. 54-55.

[12]Kelly G. Shaver, *An Introduction to Attribution Processes* (Cambridge, Mass.: Winthrop, 1975), p. 103.

[13]Lewis Carroll, *Alice's Adventures in Wonderland* (Cleveland: World, 1946), p. 77.

[14]Myers, *The Human Puzzle,* pp. 251-52.

[15]Viktor Frankl, *Man's Search for Meaning* (New York: Washington Square, 1963), pp. 172-73.

Chapter 5: Listening to Language

[1]Alan Loy McGinnis, *The Friendship Factor* (Minneapolis: Augsburg, 1979), p. 116.

[2]Ronald B. Adler and Neil Towne, *Looking Out/Looking In* (New York: Holt, Rinehart & Winston, 1984), p. 225.

[3]W. H. Crockett, A. N. Press, J. G. Delia and C. T. Kenny, "Structural Analysis of the Organization of Written Impressions," unpublished manuscript, University of Kansas, 1974.

[4]William James, *Pragmatism* (New York: Longmans, Green & Co., 1931), pp. 43-45.

[5]Lewis Carroll, *Through the Looking Glass* (New York: MacMillan, 1889), pp. 123-24.

[6]Webster's Ninth New Collegiate Dictionary (Springfield, Mass.: Merriam-Webster, 1983), p. 1005.

[7]Dr. Seuss, *Horton Hatches the Egg* (New York: Random House, 1940), p. 165.

[8]Mike Royko, *Boss* (New York: Dutton, 1971), p. 165.

[9]Kenneth Burke, *A Rhetoric of Motives* (New York: Prentice-Hall, 1950), pp. 183-91.

[10]John C. Condon, Jr., *Semantics and Communication* (New York: MacMillan, 1966), pp. 86-87.

[11]Carl Rogers, "The Characteristics of a Helping Relationship," *Personnel and Guidance Journal* 37 (1958): 6-16.

[12]Leo Tolstoy, *War and Peace,* vol. 3 (London: Oxford University Press, 1941), pp. 402-3.

Chapter 6: Nonverbal Communication

[1]Albert Mehrabian, *Silent Messages* (Belmont, Calif.: Wadsworth, 1981), p. 77.

[2]Ibid., pp. 5-17.

[3]L. Edna Rogers and Richard Farace, "Analysis of Relational Communication in Dyads: New Measurement Procedures," *Human Communication Research* 1 (1975): 222-39.

[4]Adler and Towne, *Looking Out/Looking In,* p. 257.

[5]Watzlawick, Beavin and Jackson, *Pragmatics of Human Communication,* p. 59.

[6]Marianne LaFrance and Clara Mayo, "Kinesics" in *Moving Bodies* (Monterey, Calif.: Brooks Cole, 1978).

[7]Paul Ekman and Wallace V. Friesen, *Unmasking the Face* (Englewood Cliffs, N.J.: Prentice-Hall, 1975).

[8]Dale Leathers, *Successful Nonverbal Communication* (New York: MacMillan, 1986), pp. 28-41.

[9]Michael Argyle and M. Cook, *Gaze and Mutual Gaze* (Cambridge: Cambridge University Press, 1976).

[10]Ellen Berscheid and Elaine Walster, "Physical Attractiveness," *Advances In Experimental Social Psychology,* vol. 7, ed. L. Berkowitz (New York: Academic Press, 1974), pp. 158-215.

[11]J. B. Cortes and F. M. Gatti, "Physique and Self-Description of Temperament,"

Journal of Consulting Psychology 29 (1965): 434.

[12]Proxemics. Edward Hall, *The Hidden Dimension* (Garden City, N.Y.: Doubleday, 1966).

[13]Haptics. N. M. Henley, *Body Politics: Power, Sex and Nonverbal Communication* (Englewood Cliffs, N.J.: Prentice-Hall, 1977), p. 105.

[14]Michael G. Young, "The Human Touch: Who Needs It?" *Bridges Not Walls*, 2d ed., ed. John Stewart (Reading, Mass.: Addison-Wesley, 1977), pp. 98-101.

[15]Vocalics. J. R. Davitz, *The Communication of Emotional Meaning* (New York: McGraw-Hill, 1964).

[16]Olfaction. (I've always wanted to see a perfume store called "The Olfactory.") R. W. Moncrieff, *Odour Preference* (New York: Wiley, 1966).

Chapter 7: Interpersonal Attraction

[1]L. Nahemon and M. P. Lawton, "Similarity and Propinquity in Friendship Formation," *Journal of Personality and Social Psychology* 32 (1975): 204-13.

[2]"When I'm Not Near the Girl I Love" from *Finian's Rainbow*. Lyrics by E. Y. Harburg.

[3]"I've Grown Accustomed to Her Face" from *My Fair Lady*. Book and lyrics by Alan Jay Lerner.

[4]R. B. Zajonc, "Attitudinal Effects of Mere-Exposure," *Journal of Personality and Social Psychology* 9, Monograph supplement (1968): pp. 1-29.

[5]Stanley Schachter, *The Psychology of Affiliation* (Stanford: Stanford University Press, 1959), pp. 1-19.

[6]"The Farmers and the Cowboys" from *Oklahoma*. Book and lyrics by Oscar Hammerstein II.

[7]C. Hovland and R. Sears, "Minor Studies in Aggression: Correlations of Lynchings with Economic Indices," *Journal of Psychology* 9 (1940): 301-10.

[8]Muzafer Sherif, O. J. Harvey, B. Jack White, William Hood and Carolyn Sherif, *Intergroup Conflict and Cooperation: The Robbers Cave Experiment* (Norman, Okla.: University of Oklahoma Institute of Intergroup Relations, 1961).

[9]Elaine Walster, Vera Aronson, Darcy Abrahams and Leon Rottman, "Importance of Physical Attractiveness in Dating Behavior," *Journal of Personality and Social Psychology* 5 (1966): 508-16.

[10]R. J. Pellegrini, "Impressions of Male Personality as a Function of Beardedness," *Psychology* 10 (1973): 29-33.

[11]W. J. Cahnman, "The Stigma of Obesity," *Sociological Quarterly* 9 (1968): 283-99.

[12]Chris L. Kleinke, *First Impressions* (Englewood Cliffs, N.J.: Prentice-Hall, 1975), p. 16.

[13]Elliot Aronson, *The Social Animal*, 2d ed. (San Francisco: W. H. Freeman, 1972), pp. 230-32.

[14]Donn Byrne, *The Attraction Paradigm* (New York: Academic Press, 1971), pp. 50-52.

[15]Zick Rubin, *Liking and Loving* (New York: Holt, Rinehart and Winston, 1973), p. 143.

[16]E. O. Laumann, "Friends of Urban Men: An Assessment of Accuracy in Reporting

Their Socioeconomic Attributes, Mutual Choice, and Attitude Agreement," *Sociometry* 32 (1969): 54-69.

[17]Robert E. Winch, *Mate Selection: A Study of Complementary Needs* (New York: Harper & Row, 1958), pp. 245-48.

[18]Edmund Bergler, *Divorce Won't Help* (New York: Harper & Bros., 1948), p. 11.

[19]Jonathan L. Freedman and David O. Sears, "Selective Exposure," *Advances in Experimental Social Psychology* 2 (1965): 57-97.

[20]Melvin J. Lerner, "The Desire for Justice and Reactions to Victims," *Altruism and Helping Behavior*, ed. J. Macaulay and L. Berkowitz (New York: Academic Press, 1970).

[21]Aronson, *The Social Animal*, pp. 223-26.

[22]Kleinke, *First Impressions*, pp. 113-22.

[23]Dale Carnegie, *How to Win Friends and Influence People* (New York: Pocket Books, 1972), p. 31.

[24]Edward Jones, *Ingratiation* (New York: Appleton-Century-Crofts, 1964).

[25]D. G. Dutton and A. J. Arrowood, "Situational Factors in Evaluation Congruency and Interpersonal Attraction," *Journal of Personality and Social Psychology* 18 (1971): 222-29.

[26]David Landy and Elliot Aronson, "Liking for an Evaluator as a Function of His Discernment," *Journal of Personality and Social Psychology* 9 (1968): 133-41.

[27]Elliot Aronson and Darwin Linder, "Gain and Loss of Esteem as Determinants of Interpersonal Attractiveness," *Journal of Experimental Social Psychology* 1 (1965): 156-71.

[28]Jon Jecker and David Landy, "Liking a Person as a Function of Doing Him a Favor," *Human Relations* 22 (1969): 371-78.

Chapter 8: Trust and Transparency

[1]Irwin Altman and Dalmas Taylor, *Social Penetration* (New York: Holt, Rinehart and Winston, 1973).

[2]Em Griffin, "Communication Patterns in Four Types of Intimate Friendship," presented at 1983 Speech Communication Association, Washington, D.C.

[3]"Being" scale of Caring Relationship Inventory, Educational and Industrial Testing Service, San Diego, Calif.

[4]Julian Rotter, "Trust Everybody, But Cut the Cards," *Psychology Today*, October 1980, p. 32.

[5]Rotter, "Trust Everybody," pp. 38-40.

[6]Mary Brown Paralee, "The Friendship Bond," *Psychology Today*, October 1979, p. 53.

[7]Keith Miller, *A Question of Intimacy* (film produced by U M Com Productions, Nashville, 1981).

[8]Em Griffin, *Getting Together* (Downers Grove, Ill., InterVarsity Press, 1982), pp. 125-26.

[9]Elaine Hatfield, "The Dangers of Intimacy," *Communication, Intimacy and Close Relationships*, ed. Valerian Derlega (Orlando: Academic Press, 1984), pp. 207-20.

[10]Miller, *A Question of Intimacy.*

[11]Lynn C. Miller and John Berg, "Selectivity and Urgency in Interpersonal Exchange," *Communication, Intimacy and Close Relationships,* pp. 161-205.

[12]Alan Loy McGinnis, *The Friendship Factor* (Minneapolis: Augsburg, 1979), p. 42.

[13]Sidney M. Jourard, *The Transparent Self* (New York: D. Van Nostrand, 1971), pp. 213-17.

[14]Sidney M. Jourard, *Self-Disclosure* (New York: John Wiley & Sons, 1971), pp. 78-88.

[15]Mark L. Knapp, *Interpersonal Communication and Human Relationships* (Boston: Allyn and Bacon, 1984), pp. 30-58.

Chapter 9: Accountability and Forgiveness

[1]Rollo May, *Love and Will* (New York: W. W. Norton, 1969), pp. 276-86.

[2]Jim Wallis, *Agenda for Biblical People* (New York: Harper & Row, 1976), pp. 78-99.

[3]Frederick Buechner, *Godric* (New York: Harper & Row, 1983), p. 7.

[4]Antoine de Saint-Exupery, *The Little Prince,* trans. Katherine Woods (New York: Harcourt, 1943), p. 71.

[5]Jacob M. Braude, *Complete Speaker's and Toastmaster's Library,* vol. 3: *Definitions and Toasts* (Englewood Cliffs, N.J.: Prentice-Hall, 1965), p. 31.

[6]Lewis B. Smedes, *Forgive and Forget* (San Francisco: Harper & Row, 1984), p. 2.

[7]Ibid., pp. 1-37.

[8]I'd like to acknowledge the invaluable assistance of Melinda Rynbrandt in this research. Although I located the participants, it was to Melinda that they poured out their stories. Without her approachable manner and sensitive ear, this study would not have happened.

[9]*Country,* © 1984 Buena Vista Distribution Co., Inc.

[10]David Augsburger, *Caring Enough To Forgive* (Ventura, Calif.: Regal Books, 1981), pp. 68-76.

[11]Frederick Buechner, *Wishful Thinking: A Theological ABC* (New York: Harper & Row, 1973), pp. 26-27.

[12]Alan Jay Lerner, *My Fair Lady* (New York: Coward-McGann, 1956). Used by permission of Chappel & Co.

Chapter 10: The Friendship Mandate

[1]C. S. Lewis, *The Four Loves* (New York: Harcourt Brace Jovanovich, 1960), pp. 87-88.

[2]Bruce Larson, *The Relational Revolution* (Waco, Tex.: Word Books, 1976), p. 91.

[3]Martin Buber, "Elements of the Interhuman," trans. Roger Gregor Smith, *Bridges Not Walls,* 2d ed., ed. John Stewart (Reading, Mass.: Addison-Wesley, 1977), pp. 280-92.

[4]Em Griffin, "Communication Patterns."

[5]Keith Davis, "Near and Dear: Friendship and Love Compared," *Psychology Today,* February 1985, pp. 22-30.

[6]Lewis, _Four Loves,_ p. 91.

[7]Frederick Buechner, _Sacred Journey_ (San Francisco: Harper & Row, 1982), p. 70.

[8]Gordon Chelune, Joan Robison and Martin Kommer, "A Cognitive Interactional Model of Intimate Relationships," _Communication, Intimacy, and Close Relationships,_ ed. Valerian J. Derlega (Orlando: Academic Press, 1984), pp. 11-40.

[9]Teilhard de Chardin, quoted in McGinnis, _The Friendship Factor,_ p. 192.

Further Reading

Interpersonal Communication
  Adler, Ronald and Towne, Neil, *Looking Out/Looking In*. New York: Holt, Rinehart and Winston, 1987.
Self-Concept
  Elkins, Dov Peretz, ed., *Self-Concept Sourcebook*. Rochester, N.Y.: Growth Associates, 1979.
Motivation
  McClelland, David C., *Human Motivation*. Glenview, Ill.: Scott Foresman, 1985.
Perception
  Schneider, David, Hastorf, Albert, and Ellsworth, Phoebe, *Person Perception*. Reading, Mass.: Addison-Wesley, 1979.
Listening
  Floyd, James J., *Listening: A Practical Approach*. Glenview, Ill.: Scott Foresman, 1985.
Language
  Condon, John C., *Semantics and Communication*, 3rd ed. New York: Macmillan, 1984.
Nonverbal Communication
  Mehrabian, Albert, *Silent Messages*, 2nd ed. Belmont, Calif.: Wadsworth, 1981.
Attraction
  Berscheid, Ellen and Walster, Elaine, *Interpersonal Attraction*, 2nd ed. Reading, Mass.: Addison-Wesley, 1978.
Trust
  Gibb, Jack R., *Trust: A New View of Personal and Organizational Development*. La Jolla, Calif.: Omicron, 1978.
Transparency
  Powell, John, *Why Am I Afraid to Tell You Who I Am?* Niles, Ill.: Argus Communications, 1969.
Accountability
  Arnett, Ronald C., *Dwell in Peace: Applying Nonviolence to Everyday Relationships*. Elgin, Ill.: Brethren Press, 1980.
Forgiveness
  Smedes, Lewis B., *Forgive and Forget*. San Francisco: Harper & Row, 1984.
Friendship
  McGinnis, Alan Loy, *The Friendship Factor*. Minneapolis: Augsburg, 1979.